IMAGES OF ENGLAND

HULL PUBS AND BREWERIES

HENWOOD'S MINERVA HOTEL
WINE & SPIRIT VAULTS
R. HOOD HAGGIE & SON
MINERVA WINE & SPIRIT VAULTS

IMAGES OF ENGLAND

HULL PUBS AND BREWERIES

PAUL GIBSON

TEMPUS

This book is dedicated to my patient partner Gail and to the memory of Gertie and Rita, greatly missed canine companions on our visits to Hull's pubs.

Frontispiece: The Minerva Hotel, Nelson Street was established in 1829 when the first licensee advertised in the Hull press: 'Minerva Hotel – R. Cortis thanks public for their support after opening his house – beds are newly fitted up for their accommodation. Good fires will be kept, and attendance given on early tides, to suit all Steam Packets. He has also laid in a stock of superior old wines, spirits etc. Trusting from every attention to their comfort he will insure their future favours'. The popular house expanded to take in the adjoining property in 1831 and by 1851 a tap – the Minerva Wine & Spirit Vaults had been constructed to the north side. The tap and the hotel can be seen in this extremely rare image from around 1890; more recently the site of the former tap has been used as a brewery, which closed in 1994 and is now part of the restaurant facilities at the pub.

First published 2004
Reprinted 2006

Tempus Publishing Limited
The Mill, Brimscombe Port,
Stroud, Gloucestershire, GL5 2QG
www.tempus-publishing.com

British Library Cataloguing in Publication Data.
A catalogue record for this book is available from the British Library.

ISBN 0 7524 3284 2

Typesetting and origination by Tempus Publishing Limited.
Printed in Great Britain.

Contents

Acknowledgements

While the vast majority of the images in this book are from the author's collection, he would also like to thank all those kind colleagues and friends who have loaned material from their collections and helped with information, with special thanks to Graham Wilkinson, Sam Allon (Contracts) Ltd, Peter Allsop, Robert Burn, Bob Burton, Memory Lane Photographic Galleries, Geoff Percival, Kevin Rymer, David Smith and the staff of the Hull Local Studies Library, Allan Sykes, Martin Taylor and the staff of the Hull City Archives, John Wyles.

Bibliography

Aldabella, Pat and Barnard, Robert; East Yorkshire Local History Society, Beverley; *Hull and East Yorkshire Breweries*; 1997

Barnard, Robert; Hutton Press and Hull College of Further Education, Cherry Burton; *Barley, Mash and Yeast: A History of the Hull Brewery Company 1782 – 1985*; 1990

Barnard, Robert; Hull College Local History Unit; *Moors' & Robson's Breweries Ltd – A Brief History*; 1996

Barnard, Robert; Hull College Local History Unit; *Rough Notes on Wincolmlee Pubs*; 1998

Barnard, Robert; Hull College Local History Unit; *Ale and Architecture: Four Old Town Pubs*; 1996

Clark, Peter; Longman Group, Harlow; *The English Alehouse: A Social History 1200-1830*; 1983

Falcon Publicity, Croydon; *Illustrated History of the Hull Brewery Co. Ltd*; 1960

Gibson, Paul and Wilkinson, Graham; Kingston Press, Hull; *Lost Pubs of Hull*; 1999

Girouard, Mark; Yale University Press, London; *Victorian Pubs*; 1984

Gleadow, Major R.W.; BK Design Associates, Hull; *Hull Brewery Horses*; 1971

Jennings, Paul; Keele University Press, Keele; *The Public House in Bradford 1770-1970*; 1995

Pevsner, Nikolaus and Neave, David; Penguin Books, London; *The Buildings of England; Yorkshire – York and The East Riding*; 1995

Sykes, W.; Reprinted from the Hull and East Yorkshire Times; Malet Lambert History Society, Hull; *A History of the Streets of Hull*; 1915

Tames, Richard; Shire Publications, Risborough; *The Victorian Public House*; 2003

Wilkinson, Graham (work in progress); Hull; *Landlord*; 2004

Wilson Smith, John (unpublished), Hull; *The Inns of Holderness and Taverns of East Hull*; 1953

Introduction

Which is the oldest pub in Hull? This is a question that frequently arises when local pub enthusiasts meet to chat over a pint and has many possible answers depending on your approach to the subject. However, as is often the case, it is the question itself, which is most entertaining. Very often finding the answer to a question is something of an anticlimax, but I hope this book may give you some clues to help you come to your own conclusion. Great pleasure can be had from searching for old images and plans of pubs, and of course by visiting the pubs themselves. The surviving bricks and mortar of an old pub are tangible reminders of days gone by, and very often tell their own story. Undertaking this research returns you to a time when pubs were a feature on almost every street in Hull and virtually everyone had cause to visit them regularly, often on a daily basis.

It follows that the oldest pubs should be within the oldest areas of the city and as a general rule this is true for Hull; within the Old Town are the oldest surviving examples. As Hull's population grew the town expanded beyond its old walls into the Georgian New Town and the area now accepted as the town centre features many pubs from around 1800 onwards. Here you will find Hull's most elaborate survivals from the gin palace era of the late Victorian and early Edwardian age. Beyond the town centre are surviving examples from every other decade and generally speaking, as you move away from town centre the younger the pubs are. Exceptions do occur where buildings once isolated within outlying districts and hamlets have been incorporated into the city borough and the old buildings have survived. Good examples can be found in the excellent early ale and beerhouses of Drypool and Stepney.

The study of local and family history is booming and it is to be hoped that this renewed interest in all things old will create a better understanding of our architectural heritage and the importance of its survival. With this in mind I have attempted to illustrate a wide cross section of Hull's public houses and their links to other aspects of our history. The brief architectural chronology in Chapter One presents a starting point for examining the development and changing face of our pubs. I think many would be surprised by the continual change in design, and the stylistic similarities from one building to another at certain periods. Chapter Two illustrates an area often overlooked but one that has direct links with the pub – the off-licence. Space permits only a pictorial glance at what is a complex subject. Evolving from the early alehouses from which people carried home their ale, through a minefield of nineteenth-century legislation, the Bottle & Jug was in many ways the origin of today's off-licence. Chapter Three presents an alphabetical look back at some (not all!) of Hull's lost drinking houses. Chapter Four features scenes from the two major Hull breweries, the Hull Brewery Co. Ltd and Moors' & Robson's Ltd. And finally, a chapter devoted to a few oddments from pub life and a few suggestions as to where you may carry out your own research.

Hull's historic pubs are, as in many other cities, constantly at risk from the modern developers. Buildings that are a valuable and irreplaceable part of our social and architectural heritage are still being damaged and demolished in the name of progress. This is a volatile topic and one prone to varying degrees of interpretation. Fortunately there is light at the end of the tunnel as many new pubs are now re-using older buildings. The Wetherspoon's chain lead the way in many respects and their conversions are worthy of praise. There have been others and even those pubs newly built appear to be taking some inspiration from the past. The bland and often out of place architecture of the 1970s pubs has been toned down in recent years and new builds usually complement their surroundings.

However, it is all too easy to become negative when discussing Hull's heritage of pub architecture. Work is ongoing and productive, with many interested amateurs working hand in hand with organisations like CAMRA, the Campaign for Real Ale. Their members began to take an interest in pub architecture as well as real ale some years ago. They have produced regional inventories of buildings requiring special protection, and many publications that are commercially available. Importantly, they are often vociferous in their condemnation of companies who attempt to modernize buildings of historical importance that should be preserved intact. Without the behind-the-scenes efforts of these unpaid enthusiasts buildings would continue to be demolished or stripped of any historical worth. Outwardly many of Hull's pubs appear to have been saved but very often it is what is lost within that is most heartbreaking. There are virtually no pub interiors in Hull that retain their original floor plan. Generations of planners have designed out the passage hatch, the Snug, Smoke Room and Bottle & Jug – once part of every pub in the town. Corporate branding has dictated that small rooms in pubs are no longer acceptable, something the customers would readily disagree with. Sadly, for all their attempts to bring the public back into the pubs, they still appear completely out of tune with public opinion.

For what is such an important aspect of any city or town's history, the public house is an area often overlooked by historians. Hull is no exception, and barring a few fleeting mentions in general historical works on the city, little real work has been produced to establish a base of knowledge in this area. Many local historians have studied the pubs of the Old Town; a daunting task, resulting in few published works. Noticeable, and worthy exceptions to this rule are the histories collated by Robert Barnard and Christopher Ketchell and the ongoing research being carried out by Graham Wilkinson. A similar picture exists for those pubs beyond the Old Town; apart from the pioneering work of John Wilson Smith in the 1950s, only a limited number of small publications exist in print. Produced by this author and others, they give a general introduction to the subject but much work needs to be done.

For those interested in learning more, there are many excellent books on the subject and its spin-offs. Most of those that are particularly useful when studying Hull are listed in the bibliography, but others worth reading include: *British Inn Signs* by Eric Delderfield, which discusses the origins of pub names and inn signs in general; *The English Inn* by Richardson & Eberlein and *Inns, Ales and Drinking Customs of Old England* by Frederick Hackwood are good general histories. Those interested in architecture could do worse than to start with *The Northumbrian Pub* by Lynn Pearson and for specifically post-Second World War pubs it is worth seeking out *The Renaissance of the English Public House* by Basil Oliver and *The Planning and Equipment of Public Houses* by Francis Yorke. Breweries are covered by many individual studies; probably the best local examples, other than those listed in the bibliography, are *Joshua Tetley & Son* by Clifford Lackey and *The History of the Tower Brewery, Tadcaster* by Will Swailes. For anyone interested in studying their own local, I would recommend they first visit the Hull College *Local History Unit* within the James Reckitt Library on Holderness Road. This is where you will find local historian Chris Ketchell, who will guide you with an overall knowledge of Hull that you would be unlikely to find elsewhere.

Always remember, there is no replacement for research in the pubs themselves. Please visit them, enjoy them, even study them but most importantly – give them your support.

Paul Gibson
May 2004

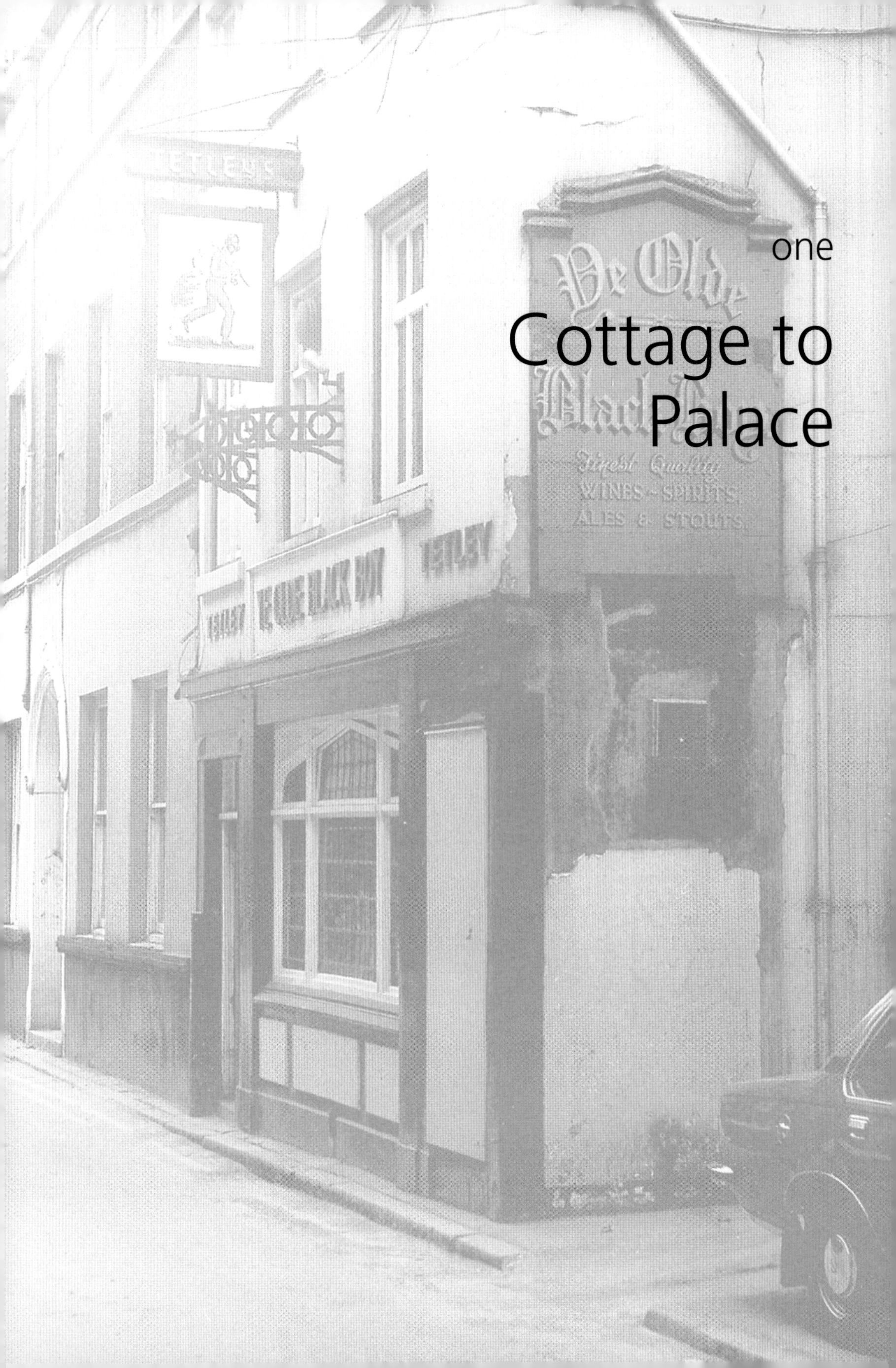

one

Cottage to Palace

Opposite: The architecture of Hull's pubs has evolved dramatically over the last two centuries. Affected by demands from the trade, legislation, and the public, pubs have grown from the simple early alehouses via the opulent Victorian gin palaces to modern functional spaces. For early images of the buildings we are mostly reliant on engravings and drawings, such as this, which shows the former King's Head Inn, High Street as it appeared in the 1870s. The property had been used as an inn during the eighteenth century, but was probably fourteenth century in origin. In one of Hull's greatest architectural tragedies the building was demolished in 1905; an act that was described as vandalism even then.

Below: The Old White Hart, situated halfway along a passage between Silver Street and Bowlalley Lane, is a 1660s Artisan Mannerist building but has only been known as a pub since around 1770. Rumours abound of events that may have taken place within its panelled walls, but few have any basis in fact. It is almost certainly the oldest existing building that is now used as a pub. This is the earliest known view from around 1860.

Early photographs of Hull's many pubs and beerhouses are extremely rare and only a small number are known to exist from the nineteenth century. Of these, possibly the best is this example from around 1890 showing two pubs on an ancient street known as North Walls. The steeply pitched roof of the Full Ship confirms its extreme age indicating it could have dated from the seventeenth century. The property line in which it stood was at one time enclosed within the Old Town walls. Its neighbour, the Scott's Head, was slightly younger – probably from around 1770. Unaware of the importance of these building in terms of Hull's heritage, they were both demolished shortly after this photograph was made.

Above: The Royal Sovereign was built around 1892 on the site of the recently demolished Full Ship and Scott's Head. Shown here in 1951, it closed on 9 December 1957 when its licence was transferred to the newly built Ravenser, Southcoates Lane.

Right: The Dog & Duck, at No.84 High Street, was another very old pub. Recorded from around 1800 in trade directories, it had probably been a pub for many years prior to this and was known to have had its own brewhouse. Situated on the east side of High Street it had not always stood on a corner. Originally part of a terrace, the property to its right, which included another pub called the General Elliott, was taken down around 1863-64 to provide access to the South Bridge (Ha'penny Bridge), constructed in 1865. The pub is shown here just before closure around 1908.

Generally speaking there are no new pubs within Hull's Old Town. Most are of long standing or are re-fronts of older buildings. The Blue Bell, situated down a passage off the Market Place has been a pub continually since at least 1791. Parts of the building may be a great deal older, as it follows a seventeenth-century property line. It is difficult to see the building now, as it is surrounded by buildings on all sides, but a rare glimpse can be had from this 1940s photograph.

The old Corn Exchange pub on North Church Side is probably created from the remains of three properties that all had links to one another: the original Corn Exchange pub, entered from a passage at No.50 Market Place; a pub known as the Excise Coffee House, which fronted North Church Side and a Wine & Spirit stores next door. Licensed as a pub from around 1780 it is shown here in the 1940s. The present building contains an original Georgian frontage on North Church Side.

A large coaching inn known as the George Hotel was once situated on the north side of Whitefriargate; an ancient establishment dating back centuries. The stables to the rear were reached via the Land of Green Ginger where a small vaults or tap of the hotel was situated. The entire hotel was rebuilt at the beginning of the nineteenth century, but its large Whitefriargate section closed in 1932; the stable entrance survives and is now known as the George pub retaining its coach entry and bootboy's lookout room and small window.

Right: The building housing the Black Boy pub in High Street is of an undetermined age, but is likely to be of the eighteenth century. The name Black Boy appears around 1738 when the building is mentioned in the deeds of an adjoining property. Originally occupying only the rear of the present building the Black Boy was not listed as a pub in several periods of the nineteenth century and only seems to reappear around 1929. However, it is not inconceivable that the pub has been licensed in one form or another for almost 270 years.

Below: The Burlington Tavern is a good example of a Georgian corner pub. Externally it retains much of its original late eighteenth-century frontage, with minor alterations to the ground floor. Originally standing at the corner of Manor Street and Broadley Street, following the construction of Alfred Gelder Street from 1901, Broadley Street was demolished, but the pub survived and is probably the only pub in the Old Town with its toilets upstairs. It is shown here around 1950.

Above: The Vauxhall Tavern at No.1 Hessle Road is one of few pubs left in Hull with Regency style details and its bow windows are typical of its period. Built around 1810 it is also Hessle Road's oldest surviving pub. It is shown here in 1926 when it was also known as Paddison's Spirit Vaults.

Right: Edgar Street was laid out in 1802 and the Barrel Tavern was listed from around 1810. From the middle of the nineteenth century, pubs, often little more than houses with hanging signs, were re-fronted to make them stand out in the streets. The Barrel is a good example of this and a rare survivor in an area decimated by redevelopment and industry. Shown here in 1926, the pub closed in 1980 and is currently in use as a café.

The Victoria Dock Tavern was constructed in the late 1820s, possibly by Simon Cook, who was listed as the first known victualler around 1830. Its original address was Drypool Square when this area was a hamlet built around the ancient church of St Peter, and quite separate from the town of Hull. First known as the Albion (a ship's name) it was renamed following the opening of Victoria Dock in 1850. A deceptive pub, it is much larger inside than one would expect.

The Duke of Edinburgh is another of Drypool's excellent clutch of early pubs. Built around 1830 it was first known as The Gate and stood on the corner of De La Pole Place and De La Pole Street. Following the extension of Great Union Street, which ran over De La Pole Street, the pub now stands alone. The Duke and its neighbours are kept in business by popular weekend pub crawls around the area and a huge increase in new housing nearby.

Queen's Road had only just been laid out when this pub was first listed in 1867 in the trade directories as the Oddfellow's Arms. Purpose built as a pub around 1866 the premises became known as the St John's Hotel around 1890 and is unusual in Hull as it retains much of its original layout of small rooms. A winner of awards for its beer and friendliness it was granted Listed Building status in 2003.

The hamlet of Dairycoates at the west end of the Hessle Road was still relatively rural when a beerhouse opened around 1872 to serve the expanding population of railway workers in the district. Standing on the corner of Chalk Lane (now Hawthorne Avenue) it is still known today as Miller's, after landlord James Miller, who was licensee at the beginning of the twentieth century. The beautiful, tiled anchor logo of the former Hull Brewery Co. is part of its ceramic tiled exterior which dates from around 1890.

The Plimsoll's Ship Hotel on the south side of Witham stands alone, a rare survivor in an area that has no private housing. Recorded from around 1815 as the Ship Inn, the property was re-fronted around 1874 when it became the Plimsoll's Ship Hotel. Sadly, the pub was neglected in the 1970s but had major renovations, including a remodelled front, in 1987. It is now the star in an otherwise dull street.

The Kingston Hotel at the corner of Trinity House Lane has its origins in a small beerhouse called the Windmill Inn, first mentioned around 1803. The Windmill closed in 1874 and the site was incorporated into a large new establishment that took in other properties on the corner. The Kingston Hotel opened in 1877, and may be one of the first purpose-built pubs in the Old Town. Its ornate, Italianate style (the architect was William Marshall of Wright Street) signalled a new era of pub architecture in Hull; first seen in London in the 1850s. The gin palace style took a while to find its way up north and the hotel is seen here in the 1960s.

The Criterion was built for local wine and spirit merchant J.R. Willford, in the gin palace style, around 1878. Its decorative brickwork is almost twinned by the Halfway Hotel further west along the Hessle Road. Purchased by the Hull Brewery Co. in 1890 it was valued at £10,000 – a huge sum of money for the time. Shown here in 1926 it continues to trade in 2004. Another surviving Willford's gin palace on the Hessle Road is the Star & Garter of 1878.

Left: The Halfway Inn was recorded on the new Hessle Road from around 1863. Wine and spirit merchant J.R. Willford bought the old cottage in around 1874 and rebuilt it as the Halfway Hotel, shown here in 1926. Also in the gin palace style, it was designed by Wm Marshall, architect of the Kingston Hotel (see p 21). The Halfway Hotel is extremely similar in style to the Criterion.

Below: A licensed house of some kind had been situated at the corner of Cleveland Street (originally Wilmington Lane) and Glass House Row since the 1830s. Currently known as the White Room, the present building is a rebuilt-structure of the 1870s and features one of the earliest glazed-tile fronts of any public house in Hull. Shown here in its prime in 1926, the pub has been sadly neglected for some years, but is now becoming popular as a live music venue.

The corner of George Street and Savile Street had been the site of a wine and spirit merchant since the 1830s and was acquired by Henry Wilson & Son around 1850. New offices were built in Savile Street in the 1870s and Hull's gin palace architecture moved up a gear when this elegant matching building was constructed in 1894. Replacing the original pub, this was to be the retail showroom of the company. Built to semi-Gothic designs of architects Smith & Brodrick, over the years it became known as Wilson's corner and from the 1950s has been known as the Dram Shop. It is now a listed building and contains ornate plasterwork and probably the only surviving horseshoe bar in Hull. It is shown here around 1905.

There has been a pub on the site of the Whittington since around 1810. It originally fronted onto Castle Street and is now situated on Commercial Road after a nineteenth-century road widening and renaming scheme. The present, vaguely Renaissance style, house is a rebuild of 1902. The building, once part of a long terrace, now stands isolated on a busy road interchange and is overshadowed by a modern shopping complex. Seen here in 1926 it remains one of Hull's most handsome pubs.

The old Punch Hotel had been situated in Waterhouse Lane since the 1840s, but was turned around to face St John's Street when rebuilt in 1895-96. Now overlooking Victoria Square it has possibly Hull's most elaborate pub frontage. Designed by Smith, Brodrick & Lowther on behalf of the Hull Brewery Co., it is a masterpiece of terracotta and *Burmantoft's* faience panels. Recognised as a listed building, the Punch is an architectural gem.

The Hessle Road Inn was renamed the Alexandra during the 1860s and rebuilt in 1895 by the Hull Brewery Co. to take in the whole corner of Ropery Street. It is a masterpiece of Victorian pub design by architects Smith, Brodrick & Lowther, as shown in this 1926 photograph.

From 1898 Clarence Street was extended to connect Great Union Street with the Holderness Road and it was at this time that the Windmill Hotel, established in the eighteenth century, was rebuilt as we see it today. A unique example of tiled gin palace architecture, it is one of Hull's listed pubs.

Above and left: The old Dock Tavern had stood in Junction Place on the south side of Queen's Dock since the 1790s. A small tough beerhouse at the dockside, it was renamed the Empress around 1876 and rebuilt during the 1890s. The later construction of Alfred Gelder Street from 1902 required some of the buildings in Junction Place, including the Empress, to be set back. Following compulsory purchase the 1890s frontage was removed, and the Empress was redesigned with a new smoke room set under the warehouse at its rear, more than doubling its capacity. The old 1890s front is shown here in a somewhat poor but extremely rare image, and in comparison the new 1903 building with modern extension is shown as we see it today.

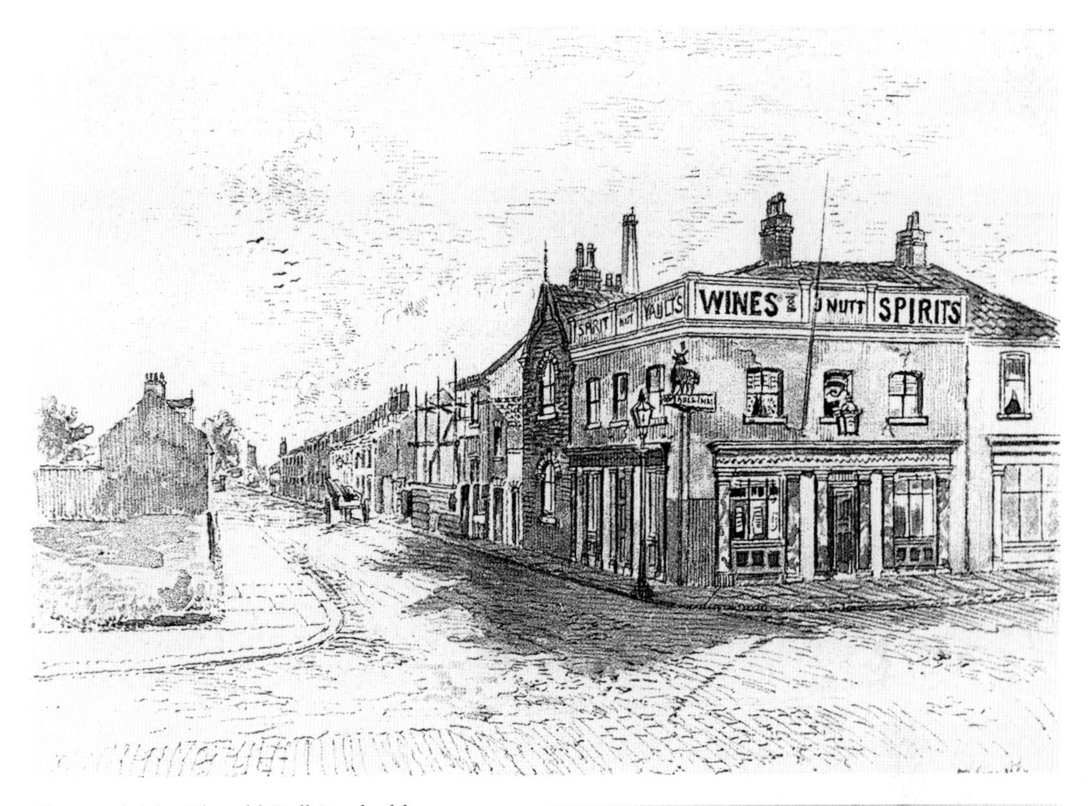

Above and right: The old Bull Inn had been a staging post for coaches on the road from Hull to Beverley and York since the late 1700s. The above drawing by local artist F.S. Smith shows the original building, at the corner of Stepney Lane around 1882. Moors' & Robson's rebuilt the dilapidated building during 1903 and 1904 in the splendid gin palace style we see today. The attention to detail on the Bull Inn has to be seen close up to be appreciated and is shown here shortly after the rebuild. The gilded bull still looks down on passers by today, although it is probably not the original model.

Above and left: The White Hart is an excellent example of Hull's many surviving gin palace-style pubs. Originally a small building fronting Salthouse Lane it has held a licence since around 1800 or earlier. Due to the construction of Alfred Gelder Street (1902-05), which cut through the property to the south of Salthouse Lane, the White Hart was rebuilt around 1904 and extended back to meet the new street. A grand south-facing frontage was built and the old beerhouse area, now at the rear, was incorporated into the new building. Its exterior and some internal details are amongst Hull's most impressive. Shown, right, shortly after opening and in a wider 1920s view above.

The Lockwood Arms, in Green Lane opened around 1870 and in 1914 the Hull Brewery Co. re-built the beerhouse as a larger hotel. Following a campaign by pub enthusiasts the building was awarded Listed Building status in 1998; its faience-tiled exterior being unique in Hull. It is now known as the Bull & Bush.

The Sandringham House has been a pub since around 1863. Its subtle half-timbered frontage was applied in 1921; this and many surviving internal details are from this date. Shown here in the 1940s the pub has so far resisted being themed, as has been the misfortune of many pubs in this popular area of the city centre.

The Albion Hotel, Caroline Street was established around 1850 and acquired by Hull Brewery Co. in 1920. This is likely to be the date of the unique faience exterior, almost certainly designed by Freeman, Son & Gaskell. Its pillars and grapevine details are architectural gems in an otherwise workaday area.

Established in the mid-nineteenth century, the Engineers Arms in Gibson Street was enlarged by the Hull Brewery Co. in 1925 by extending the building (originally set back from the road) to the street line. The rather low-key work is at odds with more extravagant buildings of the same period such as the Albion and the Sandringham.

Above and below: The original Haworth Arms was built just beyond the Newland Toll Bar on the Beverley Road around 1800 and was first recorded as a pub in the 1820s. It had many titles before being named as the Haworth Arms around 1840. The junction on which the old pub (shown here around 1905) was situated was inadequate for the increasing levels of traffic and in 1926 the whole crossroads was redeveloped. The old Haworth was demolished after the new pub was built immediately behind as the photograph below shows. Opened in 1927 the Haworth Arms is now a listed building.

West Street was laid out in 1788 and was populated by mainly immigrant Irish families. A mixture of two- and three-storey housing, some had closed courts at the rear. Only three houses facing South Street had gardens. One of these became a beerhouse around 1870 known as the Star of the West. It was probably at that time that it extended over its former garden to form the bar area, as shown in this photograph from around 1926.

In 1928 the Hull Brewery extended the pub again, this time vertically! This photograph shows the new front in the imitation half-timbering that was fashionable at the time. Pictured in the 1960s, the pub was demolished in 1997 for the extension of the Prospect Shopping Centre.

Top and above: The Goodfellowship Inn on Cottingham Road was constructed when all around was still open fields. Built in 1928 it was almost a folly of imitation half-timbering, mock-Tudor chimneys and ornate bargeboards. Drawing together details from all the other similar pubs of the period it was built to serve middle class suburbia, complete with bowling green to the rear. Although much altered the pub remains very popular. Shown here in the 1930s.

Above: Moors' & Robson's had their own house styles as is shown by this 1950s photo of the Anlaby Park Hotel. Built in 1934 it typifies their 1930s pub design with Art Deco styling and simple clean lines. Another very similar building is the Avenue on Chanterlands Avenue of the same year. The Anlaby Park is still a very popular local although much altered.

The Grapes Inn was recorded in Sykes Street from around 1806. Originally a small two-bay house it was extended around 1830 and in 1841 was described as 'five lodging rooms, 2 sitting rooms, a tap room, good cellars, an excellent brewery – well equipped with water, and free from brewer and spirit merchant'. These additions can be seen to the right of the three-storey building in the photograph of around 1926 (*opposite below*). The Grapes was demolished late in 1935 and during the rebuilding works it continued to trade from a small wooden shack (*right*), thus keeping its licence. The rebuilt pub, by George Houlton & Sons for the Hull Brewery Co. is shown (*below*) in 1936. This building remains, but a recent change of owner has resulted in a change of name. In renaming the pub the Charterhouse, we lost the last Grapes in Hull.

Built for Moors' & Robson's on the Sutton New Road in 1938, the Lamwath took its name from the Lamwath Water, an ancient watercourse that ran nearby. To the right, or east, of the building is an 'out door dept' or off-licence, now sadly gone. The rear room of the pub featured Jacobean Oak panelling taken from the Anlaby Old Hall dated 1633, only recently removed. Shown here in 1938 just after opening.

The old Three Tuns had stood in Great Passage Street since the 1820s and closed following large-scale demolition in the area, in 1936. The licence was transferred to a new pub on the Boothferry Road, which opened the same year. The new building is one of many suburban roadhouse-style pubs built to serve the new housing estates of the 1920s and 1930s.

The interior of the Three Tuns' Art Deco lounge is pictured here in 1936 and shows the change from many small rooms to large, more manageable, single rooms. The pub continues to trade in 2004, but is quite different internally.

The Bridges pub was constructed in 1949 for the Hull Brewery Co. at a cost of £24,000 in a later version of the roadhouse style, shown here around 1950. The pub struggled initially but was eventually supplied with ample trade from the 1960s housing estates of Sutton Park and Bransholme.

The first Spencer Arms was built in 1931 to replace the 'Jack on a Cruise' which was demolished for Ferensway. The 1931 building was demolished following Blitz damage and this new pub was built in 1956. It is now known as Circus-Circus, a pre-club venue.

Building restrictions had been lifted by the end of the 1950s and a new style of pub emerged. Still fairly simple in terms of design, the majority were situated on new housing estates around the edge of the city. The Dart, built on Hebden Avenue in 1959 is a good example and was Longhill's first pub. Note the integral off-licence, aimed at promoting Hull Brewery Co.'s range of take-home beers.

Into the 1960s and little change in terms of architecture, as shown by the plain box structure of The Pelican on James Reckitt Avenue. Built in 1961 it was situated at the edge of what is known as 'Pelican Field', the former sports ground of G.T. Earle & Co. whose emblem was the Pelican; hence the pub's title.

The Highland Laddie, Southcoates Lane was one of around forty new pubs built after the war on land reserved for local breweries by the council in a scheme to assist local brewers who had lost properties in the war. By holding vacant land and suspending the licences of lost pubs rather than extinguishing them, locals were given a chance to regain a foothold before any out of town breweries took unfair advantage.

Many areas of new housing were constructed on the outskirts of Hull and the new pubs were constructed to serve them. Built in 1961, the Highland Laddie followed the distinct style of the late 1950s pubs with an equally austere interior.

The elaborate designs of the nineteenth century gin palace were far from the mind of the late sixties architects. The Shoulder of Mutton, Lister Street, built in 1969, was a series of simple boxes attached to each other; it was hardly inspired but of its time. Latterly a popular live music venue it was demolished in the 1990s.

Above: The Swallow on Wawne Road was possibly the last purpose-built Hull Brewery Co. pub. The brewery closed in 1972 and The Swallow was completed early in that year. With its unique hexagonal design and integral off-licence it was a marked improvement on the designs of the late 1960s.

Right: An encouraging new trend is the reuse of older buildings; former banks, shops and even cinemas have recently been converted into popular pubs. An example from the Wetherspoon's chain is the Three John Scotts in Lowgate, formerly the main post office.

Ale and beerhouses have been set up in private houses for centuries and opening a pub in a building that had previously been used for another purpose is nothing new. Out of the twenty to thirty newly opened pubs in Hull in the last twenty years, less than 25 per cent have been purpose built. Obviously converting an old property is far cheaper than designing and constructing a new property. However, there have been some good purpose-built pub buildings in recent years and a well-designed example is The Royal Charter on Salthouse Road. Built to serve the new housing estate around Western Gailes Way, it shows an interesting return to the imitation half-timbering that was fashionable in the early part of the twentieth century.

two

Bottle and Jug

The Bottle & Jug area of the local pub or beerhouse was in many ways the origin of today's off-licence. As mechanical bottling advanced and legislation allowed greater freedom, off sales and sales of bottled beers in general, grew and separate premises were required. The Norwood Arms had been a beerhouse since the early 1860s at the corner of Osborne Street and Waterhouse Lane. This photograph, from around 1926, shows the Norwood with etched glass side door entrance to the Bottle & Jug Department.

TELEPHONE 4109Y9.

F. A. CHARLES, 331, HOLDERNESS ROAD, (Near Durham Street), HULL.

This advertising card was used to promote the store of Frederick Arthur Charles of No.331 Holderness Road. The card dates from around 1915 and it must surely be Mr Charles at the door. Originally No.2 Salem Terrace, this property was built around 1867 and licensed from that date, initially as an addition to a grocery store. First leased by Worthington's, it was later part of a chain of shops owned by one of Hull's few independent wines and spirit companies J.A. Wild of No.65 Durham Street. They purchased the shop in 1955 and it was granted a full beer, wine and spirits off-licence in 1961. Amazingly the store continues to trade as an off-licence and is known as The Drinks Cabin, still serving the locals after 125 years.

Left: A long time Hull Brewery Co. property, No.223 Waterloo Street held an off-licence since at least 1877. Shown here around 1914, it is almost certainly Mrs Hardman, wife of Joseph Hardman grocer and beer retailer, standing in the doorway. The shop ceased to be an off-licence in 1969 and was demolished soon after.

Below: At No.33 New George Street was James Dixon Mansell's off-licence. This was one of very few John Smith's off-licenses in Hull and a large hanging Magnet Ales sign can be seen, intended to be viewed from oblique angles all along the street. The shop had been licensed since at least 1873, but closed in 1934 and was demolished.

Right: No.51 Strickland Street had been an off-licence since at least 1878. Shown here around 1930 when Joseph Shawler was the licensee, it was predominantly a Hull Brewery Co. outlet although it also sold 'Bass No.5 in bottle, Whitbread London Stout, Guinness Stout' and several others according to its many signs. It remained an off-licence and grocers until the 1950s, when it was converted into a house.

Below: The east side of Porter Street at its junction with Adelaide Street is shown here in the early 1930s. On the corner is the ale, porter and grocery shop of Mrs Agnes Elizabeth Grasby, which had been an off-licence since around 1890. All the property shown here was demolished soon after this photograph was taken for the construction of the flats known as Melbourne House.

No.17 Lansdowne Street was a grocery store and off-licence that had been licensed since around 1870; latterly a Linsley's store, it is shown here in the 1920s. The shop closed around 1939 when the area was redeveloped and the site is now beneath the huge complex of the Hull Royal Infirmary.

No.72 Church Street, on the corner of Prior Street, was in an area of Hull known as Drypool. It stands alone in this 1950s photograph when much of the property in the area had been cleared for redevelopment. An off-licence had been held for this property since 1876 and it continued to trade into the 1960s.

Right: Williamson Street has lost most of its original property over the last thirty years and many small shops and warehouses that made up this important thoroughfare in East Hull have gone without trace. No.60 Williamson Street had been an off-licence and grocer since 1879 and is shown here in the 1950s.

Below: Raywell Street was home to the brewery of Moors' & Robson's who owned very few off-licences in the city; one of them, however, was in Raywell Street itself. Its postal address was No.7 Russell Street and it had been licensed since at least 1851. It is shown here in a 1967 photograph prior to its demolition in 1969.

The Hull Brewery Co. had owned No.43 George Street since the 1920s and No.45 had long been known as 'The Chocolate Box', a confectioners and tobacconists. Shown here in the 1960s, both were acquired by the famous Carmichaels store, which is now the site of the Ven-U nightclub and bar.

The Queen's Hotel, Queen's Road opened in the early 1870s complete with a separate Bottle & Jug area. As demand grew for bottled beers an elaborate shop front was fitted, as shown in this 1960s photograph. The off-licence closed in the 1980s, the last integral off-licence of its kind in the city.

three

Albany to Zetland

Left: The Albany, originally The Blue Bell, was a very old inn that had stood on the corner of Blue Bell Yard, off Waterworks Street (now Paragon Street), since the late eighteenth century. The Albany, shown here in the 1920s, closed on 8 May 1941 due to severe damage sustained during an air raid.

Below: Originally known as the Sculcoates Arms, this pub changed its name between 1863 and 1876 to The Albert Hotel possibly as a mark of respect to Prince Albert who had died in 1861. Situated on the corner of Scott Street and Carr Street, it closed on 17 December 1936 and was demolished soon after.

Above: This unassuming backstreet beerhouse was first recorded around 1872. Latterly a Moors' & Robson's house it was situated at No.39 Wright Street, near the corner of Reed Street. It became known as the Albemarle Inn around 1890, although the origin of the name is unclear. It closed in 1973 and the site is now beneath Freetown Way.

Right: Another example of imitation half-timbering was the Builders Hotel, Cogan Street, whose exterior redesign was completed in 1928. Having been a beerhouse since around 1817 and known as the Builders' since the 1860s, it closed in the 1970s and was demolished soon after.

It is unlikely that we shall ever see internal fixtures and fittings of this quality again. Rumours abound as to the origin of the items within the Argyle, probably just the work of skilled tradesmen at the time of its refurbishment. Sadly, their removal is as much of a mystery as their origin.

A superb mock-Tudor fire surround overlooked the long bar of the Argyle, probably inserted when the pub was refitted with its imitation half-timbering in 1927. Just one hand-pulled beer engine sits atop the counter, in stark contrast to today's rows of 'smooth', 'cold' and 'creamy' beers and lagers.

Above: Situated at the end of the long bar was this cosy corner with a simple country style fireplace. On the wall is a price list from owners Henry Wilson & Son Ltd.

Right: The Argyle Hotel was originally a private house on the south side of Anlaby Road opposite Asylum Lane but by 1858 it had become licensed premises. Asylum Lane was renamed Argyle Street in 1861 following the closure of the lunatic asylum there around 1849. The street may have been renamed after the pub, similarly to Paragon Street, which was named after the Paragon Hotel. The Argyle closed in 1965.

Left: The Cambridge Hotel, situated on the corner of Great Thornton Street and Cambridge Street, had served its locals since 1872. The pub closed on 5 February 1959 and its licence was transferred for the granting of a full licence to the Sheffield Arms, Hessle Road.

Below: The Citadel Hotel was constructed on the site of the seventeenth-century Citadel and was laid out with new streets during the 1860s. It would have been kept busy by workers from the nearby cattle yards, timber yards and docks. A large pub of four rooms it had been a Hull Brewery Co. house since 1927 and closed on 4 May 1960.

Originally a T. Linsley & Co. house, the Clarence Hotel, Charles Street did not receive a full licence until 1957. Sadly, it was lost in 1987 during large-scale demolition of the area, by which time it was a well-known Tetley house.

One of the greatest losses to Hull's historical pub architecture was this building situated on Mytongate. The Coach & Horses was one of Hull's principal coaching inns and stonework in the stables to the rear of the building was dated to 1660. Closing in 1970 it was demolished in 1973 amidst the huge folly of redevelopment in Hull's Old Town during the 1970s.

HOTEL
TETLEY'S
COMMERCIAL
HOTEL
LEY'S

HULL
BREWERY
HULL BREWERY CO. LTD
SPIRIT
HOTEL
STORES

Above: The Cromwell Hotel at No.59 Walmsley Street received its first licence in 1868. In 1876 it became a Kendall & Gruby, Exchange Brewery house and in 1892 Worthington's bought the brewery and the estate of twenty-four pubs, which included the Cromwell. Closing in the 1970s, it was demolished in the 1980s.

Opposite above: The Commercial Hotel was constructed at No.1 Castle Street around 1829. Acquiring its name around 1862, the pub front was replaced with the ubiquitous green tiled Victorian frontage around 1895. Another victim of the Mytongate demolition programme, this glorious Tetley's pub was demolished in 1981.

Opposite below: The Commercial Hotel, latterly No.57 Cogan Street is recorded from around 1840. Shown here in 1926 the small two-roomed pub later lost its grand corner doors, with their etched 'Dram Shop' glass, and was eventually demolished in the early 1970s.

Probably the most famous owners of the Cross Keys Hotel in the Market Place were the Varley family who were connected with this establishment for over sixty years, a Mrs Anne Varley being the proprietor from 1859 to 1907. The Cross Keys closed as a hotel in 1922 and by 1937 the building had become almost derelict and the decision was taken to clear the site. A newspaper article of the time described the building: 'It was a large and impressive four-storeyed building with a double front and stabling for forty horses, to the rear was the great courtyard in which hung a bell dated 1596 along with great branches of decorated ironwork from which the oil lamps swung when the steaming horses clattered in on a winters night. In one of the courtyard buildings was a lovely Georgian bow window with a doorway next to it announcing a saving bank where the farmers left their money on market days'. The area was redeveloped in the 1970s and the site of the hotel is now marked by King William House and the adjacent multi-storey car park.

Regarding the Crown Inn, Holderness Road, the minutes of the Housing and Town Planning Committee dated Feb 1927 noted: 'The City Engineer reported that negotiations had taken place with Messrs Worthington & Co. with reference to the improvement of the Holderness Road at this point and he submitted a letter from Messrs John Watson & Carter offering on behalf of the company to demolish the Crown Inn and to give the Corporation an area of 272 square yards for the road widening provided the Corporation would, in exchange therefore, give to the company an area of 453 square yards of land forming part of the site of the White Horse Farm, belonging to the committee, together with the sum of £1,000 towards the cost of the erection of the new premises.' This extract succinctly sums up the history of one current and one long-demolished Hull pub. The old Mile House had served travellers on Holderness Road since the end of the eighteenth century and is shown here in a 1920s photograph. Its replacement is one of very few examples of 1930s Art Deco pubs left in Hull.

Left: Another stylish gin palace-style pub was the Crystal Hotel, which stood at No.30 Waterloo Street. First licensed in 1868, the Crystal was demolished in the early 1970s as part of a compulsory purchase order which cleared the whole district taking with it the Sculcoates Arms, Burns Head, Mechanics Arms, Pacific Hotel and others.

Opposite above: The Earl Cardigan on Fish Street is recorded from around 1834 in trade directories. First known as the Garrick's Head and the Blue Bell, it became the Earl Cardigan around 1860. Following closure in 1957 its licence was transferred to the Wassand Arms, Wassand Street.

The first record of the Dog & Duck beerhouse, latterly No.337 Wincolmlee, was in 1830. Situated just before the junction with York Street, it was a Moors' & Robson's beerhouse from 1889, closing on 6 February 1933.

Many pubs in the densely populated area of south-west Hull served the fishermen when home from their trips at sea. The Fisherman's Arms, shown here in the 1950s, was one such pub. A Hull Brewery Co. beerhouse that stood on the corner of Adelaide Street and Goodwin Street, the pub closed in April 1958.

The Foresters Arms, latterly No.29 Finkle Street, was a property that may have dated from the 1600s. Known from around 1803 as the Blucher or Prince/General Blucher it closed in 1900 as a Moors' & Robson's house. Shown in its derelict state, complete with window shutters, in the 1960s.

The Four Alls had served travellers on the Holderness turnpike road for many years prior to its first mention in trade directories in 1840. In 1890 it became the Four in Hand, a more fitting name for its coaching history and in 1937 it was rebuilt in the mock-Tudor style we see today.

Right: The Full Measure Inn on Walton Street first opened in the 1860s and was a long-standing Moors' & Robson's house. The glazed-tile frontage was applied in 1907 during a programme of refurbishment of their properties. Latterly used as a taxi office and shown here in the 1970s, it was demolished in 1983.

Below: This rare postcard view from around 1905 looking north along Queen Street to the Market Place shows the old Golden Lion pub at No.78, to the left in the photograph. Hull was one of several cities bombed by Zeppelins in the First World War, the Golden Lion was damaged during a raid in 1915 and subsequently demolished.

Except for a brief spell when it was known as the Sheffield & Lincolnshire Railway Hotel this pub was known as the Granby Inn or Hotel throughout its life. Situated at the corner of Pier Street and Wellington Street it closed in 1941 after suffering badly in the bombing raids of 8 and 9 May that year.

Above and opposite below: I can claim a letter F for Ferry House and G for Grapes here, as this pub was known by both names prior to its re-building in 1904. It is shown here before and after. The old cobbled crossing at Stoneferry ran from Clough Road across the river Hull to Ferry Lane. The River Hull, being tidal, was crossed by a ferry at high tides and as with all ferries, there was a pub at one or both sides to accommodate the ferryman and the thirsty traveller. The ancient ferry was replaced with a magnificent new bridge in 1905 and the old Ferry House (often referred to as the 'Grapes' as its inn sign was a bunch of grapes) was demolished. In its place a huge new pub was built to the designs of Hull architects Runton & Barry. Following its opening in 1907 the house was officially renamed the Grapes Hotel. Its magnificent green-tiled frontage (shown here from around 1910) is now just a memory as it too was demolished, to make way for two new bridges in 1986.

Shown to the left in this 1904 photograph, with its hanging sign and bunch of grapes, is the Grapes Tavern, Chapel Lane. The Grapes is recorded in trade directories from 1817 and was an alehouse throughout its life. One of almost twenty pubs called the Grapes in Hull's history, the building was owned by the Hull Corporation and was early Georgian in origin. It closed on 30 December 1929 when £2,902 was paid in compensation for its closure. The building stood mostly vacant until it was demolished around 1979.

Above: No.131 Cleveland Street, the Greenland Fishery was first recorded around 1830 and became a Moors' & Robson's house from 1895. It was seriously damaged in the Blitz of 1941 and closed when compensation of £5,582 was paid. The site was later sold to Spillers Ltd for £600 and soon after demolished.

Right: Possibly the grandest bar on Carr Lane was that of the Grosvenor Hotel of around 1890. Although predominantly a large commercial and family hotel the passer-by could still pop in for a pint. It was damaged during an air raid in 1941 and was later demolished.

Left and below: William Waudby was a grocer and wine and spirits merchant at No.51 Prospect Street during the 1870s and the back room of his premises became a beerhouse from around 1880. Initially known as the Tea Canister, a reference to the shop out front, by 1900 the pub had become known as Ye Hole In Ye Wall; this may have been a reference to a serving hatch although it is more generally known to mean any pub approached by a tunnel entrance. The interior is shown here in a rare postcard view of 1914, and the exterior in another view from the early 1930s. The Hole in the Wall was destroyed in the air raids of July 1941.

Right: The grand Italianate frontage of the Imperial Hotel had dominated Paragon Street for almost a hundred years, officially opening in 1878. After surviving two world wars its bold structure was lost during the rebuilding and insensitive modernisation of the area during the 1960s.

Below: Very few pubs in Hull have begun with the letter J, and few of those appear to have been photographed. So with a little licence we have here the Horse & Jockey, Lower Union Street. Noted as a pub since at least 1814 the Horse & Jockey continued trading until around 1908 and was demolished in the 1930s.

The Blue Bell, Prospect Street was a late eighteenth-century inn that changed its name in 1876 to the Prospect Inn. In 1903 it became the King Edward VII, a Darley's house that was re-fronted in the style we see here in 1923. Shown here in the 1930s it was demolished following damage sustained in the Blitz of 1941.

The Leeds Arms in Porter Street first opened in the 1850s, and was modernised around 1936, as shown in this photograph. Having survived the Blitz of 1941 with minor structural damage, it was demolished in 1958 during redevelopment that reduced the number of licensed premises in the area from over thirty to just four.

The Leicester Hotel, Mytongate was built by joiner Edward Barker around 1790 and was first mentioned as licensed premises in 1791. In 1899 it became tied to Moors' & Robson's, where it remained until closure in 1967. The Leicester was lost around 1979 during the controversial redevelopment of Mytongate and Castle Street.

How to make the most of what you've got! The small but beautifully formed Lincoln Arms, Beaumont Street was a Hull Brewery pub that appears to have been purpose-built. Noted as a beerhouse from around 1872 it is shown here in 1926. The pub closed in 1967 and was later demolished.

From the late 1880s it was common for pubs to be re-fronted, often in brightly coloured tiles, to entice the public within. The Lord Collingwood in Lowgate was a fine example. A beerhouse (from around 1810) it was acquired by Moors' & Robson's in 1899. In 1907 they used the highest quality materials from the Burmantoft works of the Leeds Fireclay Co. to re-front the building as shown in this photograph from the late 1950s. The total cost of the works was £59 14s. Sadly all the swags, garlands and columns couldn't save it from demolition after its closure in 1959.

The demolition seen in the background of this photograph from around 1899 was clearance work in preparation for the construction of King Edward Street. Rather inconveniently, the new street was to cut straight through the smoke room of the Lord Londesborough, an old pub that had stood on this site since the 1790s. Originally called the Anchor and later the Paul Pry, it was renamed the Lord Londesborough around 1863 in honour of the colonel (honorary) of the First East Yorkshire Rifle Volunteers. At the same time (1864) the Hull Rifle Corps were given permission to name the street, which had held their Rifle Barracks, as Londesborough Street. The street leading off to the right is Savile Street, the only locating feature for this rare view.

Greengrocer Joseph Crouch was the first listed keeper of the Market Tavern, Cogan Street around 1838. It was situated at the opposite corner of Edward's Place to the aforementioned Commercial Hotel (p.58), as shown in this 1962 photograph. A long time Hewitt's of Grimsby beerhouse, it closed around 1967.

Moors' & Robson's purchased the lease of the Myton Arms in 1897 and rebuilt it as shown in this 1920s photograph. This replaced a much older beerhouse that had served the locals of Myton Street and Osborne Street since the 1840s. The pub was demolished during the 1950s.

Right: The Neptune Inn at No.49 Neptune Street, was first recorded in 1817, and owned by brewers Kendall & Gruby, until they were taken over by Worthington & Co. in 1892. The cheery local closed in 1979 but was not demolished until 1985.

Below: The Newbegin Arms, on the corner of Green Lane and Trevor Street was first recorded in the 1870s. Latterly a Worthington's house it had at one time belonged to the Victoria Brewery just over the road. The pub was demolished following closure in 1964.

Above: The original Black Horse, Carr Lane was demolished in 1941 following Blitz damage. The licence transferred to a former shop at No.6 Porter Street, shown here in the 1950s. With the transfer of the licence these premises also took on the name of the Old Black Horse and was a Hull Brewery Co. pub when it closed in 1962.

Left: Originally the Black Swan this Georgian beerhouse became known as the Old Swan around the turn of the twentieth century. Situated on Mytongate, the pub ceased trading around 1915 after which it became a lodging house and latterly the wholesale outlet for Cameron's Brewery in Hull. Seen here in the early 1960s.

Right: The Parade Hotel, a purpose-built pub, opened around 1891 at No.49 South Parade. The licence came from the Daniel O'Connell, Mill Street which closed in 1889. The Parade Hotel closed at 3 p.m. on the 4 April 1962 and the licence was transferred to the Drum & Cymbals, Sibelius Road, which opened at 6 p.m. on the same day.

Below: Despite the attempts of a committed few, our architectural heritage is still slipping slowly away. No more so than in the case of historic public houses. To make way for a new shopping complex two pubs have been demolished including this, the Providence Inn, Spring Street, which had been open since the 1840s.

Above: The Queen's Head at No.161 Walker Street opened around 1858 and closed exactly a century later on 12 June 1958. Latterly a Worthington's house it was not demolished until around 1966. It was very popular with artistes visiting the Palace Theatre and with American servicemen during the war.

Left: The Rampant Horse at Nos 9 to 11 Paisley Street opened around 1870 and was a Hewitt's beerhouse for most of its life. Rebuilt in 1895, it was to survive for just over a century, closing around 1982. It was soon demolished and the present Rampant Horse was built to replace it on Hall Road in 1982.

The Reefer was situated at the corner of Dagger Lane and Posterngate. During a programme of pub closures the Reefer was one of many in the area that were referred to a compensation committee in 1906: 'The reasons which have weighed with the Licensing Committee in selecting and reporting these licensed houses for extinguishment and payment for compensation for the licences attached thereto are as follows: Structural unsuitability for their trade on the grounds of age and other causes; The undesirable position in which such houses are situated, rendering police supervision difficult; The district is more than sufficiently supplied by the remaining licensed houses for the wants of the people living therein and visiting thereto; In the general interests of the public the renewals of the several licences reported are not desirable; The area in which these houses are situated is about 400 yards square and contains sixty-seven licensed houses.' The Reefer closed around 1910 and the building is shown here during the 1940s.

The Royal William on the corner of Waterhouse Lane and Trundle Street was another of Hull's recent losses. The fact that it was an eighteenth-century building, possibly an early brewer's house, and that it had been used as a pub since at least 1803 did nothing to prevent its demolition in August 2000.

Pasquale Anthony Rice was a popular licensee of the Royal Oak Inn, No.38 Spencer Street, hence the local name of Tony's. Shown here in a rare 1920s image the building was demolished during the construction of Ferensway in 1928-31 and rebuilt at No.2 Lombard Street. It is now known as the Yorkshireman.

Above: The Raywell Hotel was known as Tiger No.3 until 1925 when it was taken over by Moors' & Robson's, whose brewery was in Raywell Street. Situated on the corner of Cumberland Street and Wincolmlee, it was first licensed in 1874 and closed in 1960. Shown here in a rare image from around 1930.

Right and top of next page: The Ship's Hold in Wincolmlee was first recorded around 1822 and was rebuilt in 1904 when the tiled frontage shown here was applied. The door to the left of the building led to the Bottle & Jug area and the door to the right to a very small bar. The Ship's Hold closed around 1967 and was demolished in the 1970s.

Above: The Slater's Arms at No.92 West Parade is most likely to have been named with reference to the Slater family, several of whom lived in West Parade in the nineteenth century. Re-fronted in 1923 by Linsley & Co., it was latterly a Tetley's house, which closed in June 1968, two years after this photograph was taken.

It is likely to be landlord John Rhodes and his family standing at the doors of the St Leger Hotel on the corner of Paragon Street and Little Queen Street. He was landlord from 1904 until the 1920s. The St Leger was originally known as the Druids Arms and was later renamed after the famous horse race. The pub closed in 1923 but the property has been used for a number of purposes since then and is now ironically part of a pub once more. A relatively new pub Yate's recently extended to include the former old beerhouse.

Left: The Stag Inn was situated on the north side of Leonard Street. Originally a Warwick & Richardson of Newark on Trent beerhouse, the pub was first recorded in the 1860s and remained open until 1976, being demolished in the 1980s.

Below: To the right of this view from around 1905 is a beerhouse known as the Steamship Cabin, which had served the workers of the Humber Dock since the 1870s. Situated at No.13 Humber Dock Street (marked in the upper window) the pub shared its building with two other businesses on the upper floors and closed around 1906.

The Sykes Head was constructed around 1813 and was first known as the Steam Packet Tavern, a simple beerhouse, it changed its name during the 1840s. The name Sykes Head may have a connection with the famous Sykes family of Hull, mayors and wealthy merchants in the eighteenth and nineteenth centuries. The building still survives, as shown in this 1970s photograph, but has been rendered more recently and although the name board is still in place it is completely obscured.

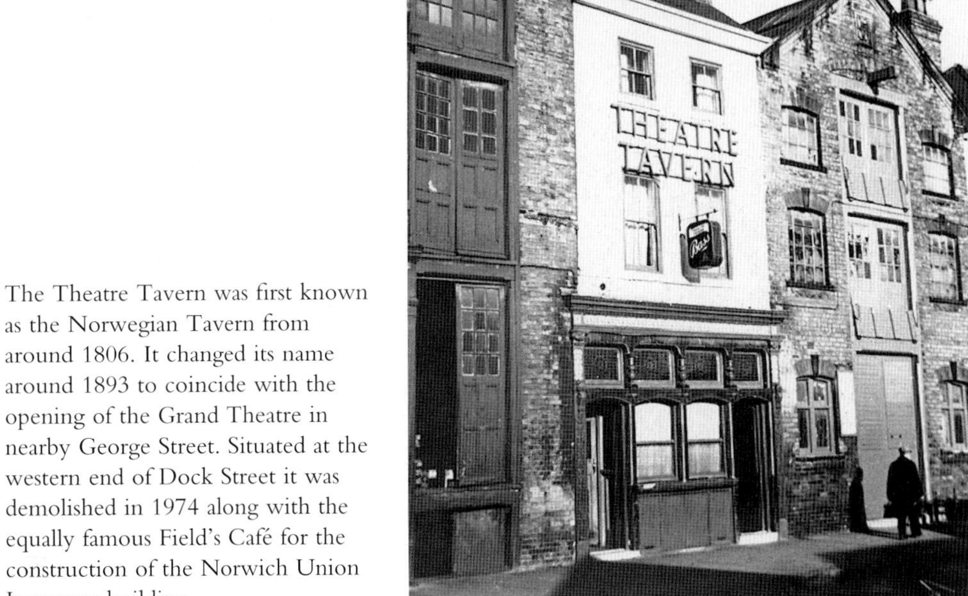

The Theatre Tavern was first known as the Norwegian Tavern from around 1806. It changed its name around 1893 to coincide with the opening of the Grand Theatre in nearby George Street. Situated at the western end of Dock Street it was demolished in 1974 along with the equally famous Field's Café for the construction of the Norwich Union Insurance building.

The Turk's Head will suffice for the letter U as well as a T in our alphabetical look back, as the few pubs that began with the letter U in Hull have gone without record. The Turk's Head was known from the early 1800s and was tied to Moors' & Robson's from 1899. The pub closed around 1908, but the building survived until redevelopment in the 1970s.

The Victoria Arms opened around 1830. It was situated on the west side of Wincolmlee, just before the junction with New George Street. During the 1880s landlord James 'Jemmy' Rawlins offered 'lessons in the noble art of Self-Defence' when 'Fistiana was always to be seen'. It is shown here around 1905 and closed on 12 January 1929.

Right: Originally known as the Victoria Gardens from around 1834, the Victoria Tavern on Chapman Street was rebuilt in 1900 in the style shown in this 1930s photograph. The expansion of the Reckitt-Benckiser Plc required the demolition of the Victoria Tavern in 2001 to create a car park entrance.

Below: Southam's Victoria Vaults, Anlaby Road was acquired by the Hull Brewery Co. in 1948, and some of their bottling was done here. The arched entry to the left led to a smoke room with a bottling area behind; to the right was the off-licence department and in the centre was the pub, which remained open until 1968.

R. KEDDEY,
Vittoria Tavern,
Water Side,
HULL.
VITTORIA TAVERN, KEDDEY

SHIPSTONE & CO.
VITTORIA HOTEL

Opposite above and below: The Vittoria Hotel was built around 1810. Mr Ralph Keddey, the first known victualler of the Vittoria Tavern, would have issued this trade card to his highly regarded customers; it shows the original Georgian building before reconstruction. The rebuilt hotel is also shown here in the 1890s; a small bar known as the Vittoria Tap was located within the hotel as it was common for grand hotels to have separate areas for the working classes to drink out of sight of the gentry.

Above and left: This inn, originally known as the Mill, had become known as the Wheatsheaf Inn by 1822, and is shown here (above) in the 1890s when Jane Moorhouse was the licensee. During the construction of King Edward Street in 1901 the building line was set back slightly, which required the reconstruction of the Wheatsheaf. The new building, shown here in 1926 (left), was also demolished without protest in 1973.

The old White Lion had stood on Collier Street since the 1830s and was demolished in 1930 to make way for a new bus station. The replacement White Lion was built in 1934 in the newly created Lombard Street. The new building, shown here in the 1960s, was demolished in July 2004, for another new bus station.

Originally known as the Tiger and later the March of Intellect, the building shown here as the Windsor, had been the site of a pub since the late 1700s. Situated at the corner of Waterworks Street and Chariot Street it is shown here in a poor but very rare 1920s photograph. It closed on 8 May 1941 following blitz damage.

Above: This 1930s photograph can be used to locate the Windsor, using the surviving Paragon Hotel to the left (now the Hull Cheese). The Windsor is to the right and the old Neptune to the top right. In the distance another lost pub – the old Brunswick at the corner of Chapel Street.

Right: The Zetland Arms, Adelaide Street opened around 1850. It was enlarged in 1912 and re-fronted in 1926 by the owners, Moors' & Robson's, as shown in this 1930s photograph. Following compulsory purchase, it closed at 3 p.m. on 25 June 1940 and its name and licence were transferred to a new pub in Portobello Street.

High Street had over fifty pubs at one time or another; sadly today there are just three. Some of its houses were of a great age and many, like this at No.168, were timber-framed, dating from the fourteenth century. Shown here as the Wilberforce Inn in 1905, this pub had been known as the Yarmouth Arms for many years prior. Possibly a pub from the 1730s, it closed in 1908. Its jettied frontage hanging out into the street was damaged in the Blitz of 1941 and remained derelict for some time. Sadly, little was done to prevent its demolition around 1950.

four

Crown and Anchor

The Hull Brewery Co. could be traced back to 1765 at a brewery in Dagger Lane and a later partnership of two Hull brewers Gleadow & Dibb. This 1911 photograph shows the Anchor Brewery, Silvester Street constructed for Gleadow & Dibb in 1868; it was they who formed the Hull Brewery Co. in 1887.

The Anchor Brewery was built on and around Silvester Street in 1868. It is shown here in 1946, with offices to the right and general warehousing to the left. All of the buildings shown here still exist and have been saved from demolition by conversion to multi-purpose occupation.

This was another Gleadow & Dibb property; constructed in 1862 it was known as Malting No.4, and was situated on Anlaby Road, west of Pease Street. The building, shown here in the 1950s, were demolished in 1966 as a more efficient drum malting had been built in Westmoreland Street in 1964.

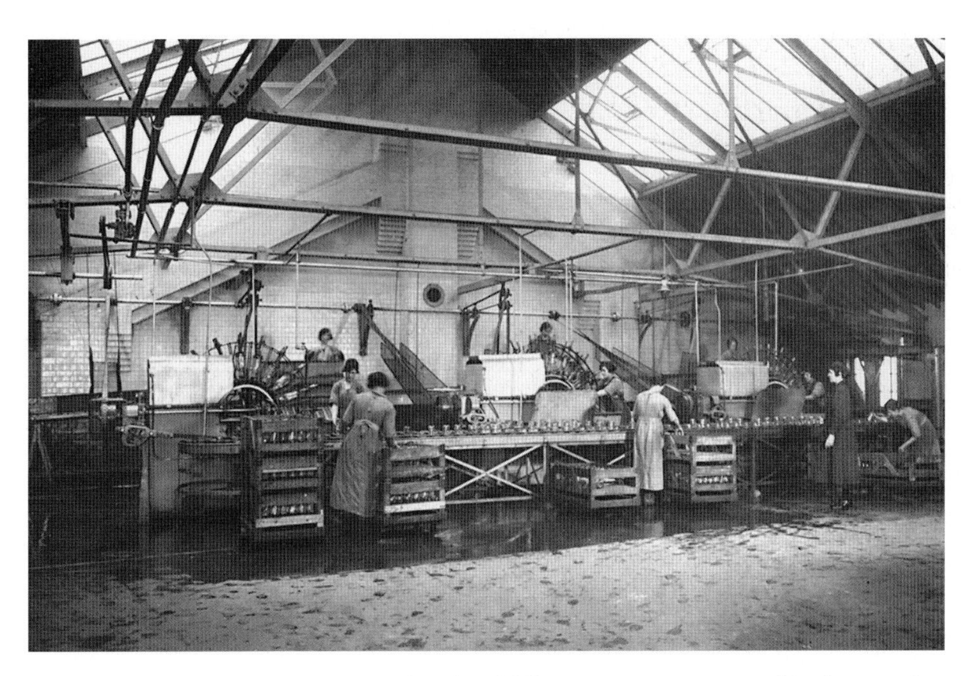

Within the Anchor Brewery was a multitude of different processing areas. This photograph from the 1920s shows the bottling or bottle cleaning plant, mainly staffed by women, in what appears to be a very labour-intensive operation.

This image from the 1960s shows bottles being washed, filled, labelled and crown corked. The 1960s plant could complete this process at a rate of anywhere between 600 and 2,000 dozen bottles per hour. Note the stylish foot wear of the still predominantly female staff.

This 1920s image shows a wines and spirits storage area, where Martini is being repacked and stored. Many spirits were blended and decanted by the company, including Anchor Blend and McBride's Mature whiskies and the famous John Peel rum. The room was probably within the Bonded Warehouse in Silvester Street.

Here we see Hull Brewery Co. Mild being packed into crates for onward despatch to the brewery's many outlets in the 1960s. In 1960 the company had 206 pubs and 39 off-licences in the Hull area alone.

This rare image shows one of the company's early horse-drawn rullies from around 1910. Its small size, drawn by a pony rather than a heavy horse, suggests that it was only used for relatively short trips within the city. It is also unusual in that it has a covered platform.

As late as the 1960s horse-drawn vehicles were still seen as economical for deliveries around the town and five horses were kept working by the Hull Brewery Co. for this purpose. Seen here delivering to the former White Lion, Lombard Street, the rully shows almost no change in design to that of 1910.

Another brewery rully, marked No.1, is shown here around 1908. Parked in the brewery yard, it is offloading sacks of raw materials via a hoist to the upper floors of the works.

The Hull Brewery Co. horses hold a place in the heart of any Hull citizen fortunate enough to have seen them moving gracefully around the city streets. This photograph from around 1915 shows (from left to right) four horses and their handlers R. Slide (stable foreman), J. Fisher, Dickey Day and Jack Winter.

Half a century later and this photograph from around 1960 shows some of the last generation of working horses at the brewery. Shown from left to right are W. I'Anson (stable foreman), 'Bob' with R. Gray, 'Lady' with A. Spencer, 'Bonny' with W. Dixon and 'Prince' with K. Taylor.

During the 1920s the company introduced a new method of beer presentation. Traditional cask conditioned beer was supplemented by chilled, carbonated and filtered products. This meant huge investment in storage and handling equipment, including large porcelain storage jars such as these shown here in the cellar of the Endyke Hotel around 1930.

To service the new storage jars a fleet of specially designed road vehicles were commissioned. This is one of the earliest, a Thornycroft tanker, registration number AT 7272, with solid wheels and wooden cab. Note the coach lamps and bulb-horn.

By the 1960s the company had five eighteen-barrel tankers, seventeen flatbed trucks and three articulated vehicles. This is one of the 1960s tankers, supplied by Cornelius Parish Ltd of Hull. The tank is mounted on an Austin 5 ton, 160 inch long wheelbase, chassis-cab.

This image was used on Hull Brewery Co. promotional material from around 1910. Shown here in the form of a postcard, it was often supplied as a framed painting to the brewery's houses. It can be seen in the window of many pubs in photographs of the period (see p.19) and shows puppies drinking Hull Brewery Co.'s celebrated XXX ale.

The Hull Brewery Co. was one of the first British breweries to put beer in cans. This display item promoting the early cans is a rare survivor from the author's collection, showing the Brasso type of tin that was used from 1949. These early tins were unsatisfactory and replaced by the more familiar flat top cans in 1954. The company was also the first to supply Marks & Spencer with canned beer.

THE

HULL BREWERY

CO., LTD.

BUDGET, 1943—REVISED PRICES.

	Bar.			Smoke Room.		
DRAUGHT ALES:	Pint.	½ Pint.		Pint.	½ Pint.	
Mild - -	1/-	6d.		1/1	6½d.	
Bitter - -	1/1½	7d.		1/2½	7½d.	
BOTTLED ALES:	Large.	Per Bottle. Small.	Nips.	Large.	Per Bottle. Small.	Nips.
H.B. Mild - -	1/1	7d.	-	1/2	7½d.	-
,, Amber - -	1/1	7d.	-	1/2	7½d.	-
,, Pale - -	1/3	8½d.	-	1/4	9d.	-
,, Double Anchor -	-	-	1/3	-	-	1/3½
Guinness Stout - -	1/7½	11d.	-	1/8½	11½d.	-
Ba.s - - -	1/10	11½d	-	1/11	1/-	-
Barclays Light Lager -	-	11d	-	-	11½d.	-

(Deposit Charge on Bottles 2d. each.)

WINES and SPIRITS.

On Sales. Bar & Smoke Room.
Whisky (all Blends) - **1/4** per measure.
Rum ,, - **1/4** ,,
Gin ,, - **1/4** ,,
Wine - increased **1**d. per Glass.
Brandy - ,, **3d.** ,,

Off Sales.
Whisky and Rum - **25/9** per bottle.
13/6 per half bottle.
Gin - - - **25/3** per bottle.
13/3 per half bottle.
Wine, Foreign and Colonial, increased **1**/- per bottle.
,, British - ,, **6d.** ,,

(Customers are requested to see that they are not charged in excess of these Prices.)

19th April, 1943.

A popular topic for discussion in pubs when older locals get together is the price of beer. Just how cheap was it? This price list from 1943 may shed some light; was it really that cheap? The Hull Brewery Co. was taken over by Northern Dairies in 1972 and re-emerged as the North Country Brewery who were in turn bought by Mansfield in 1985.

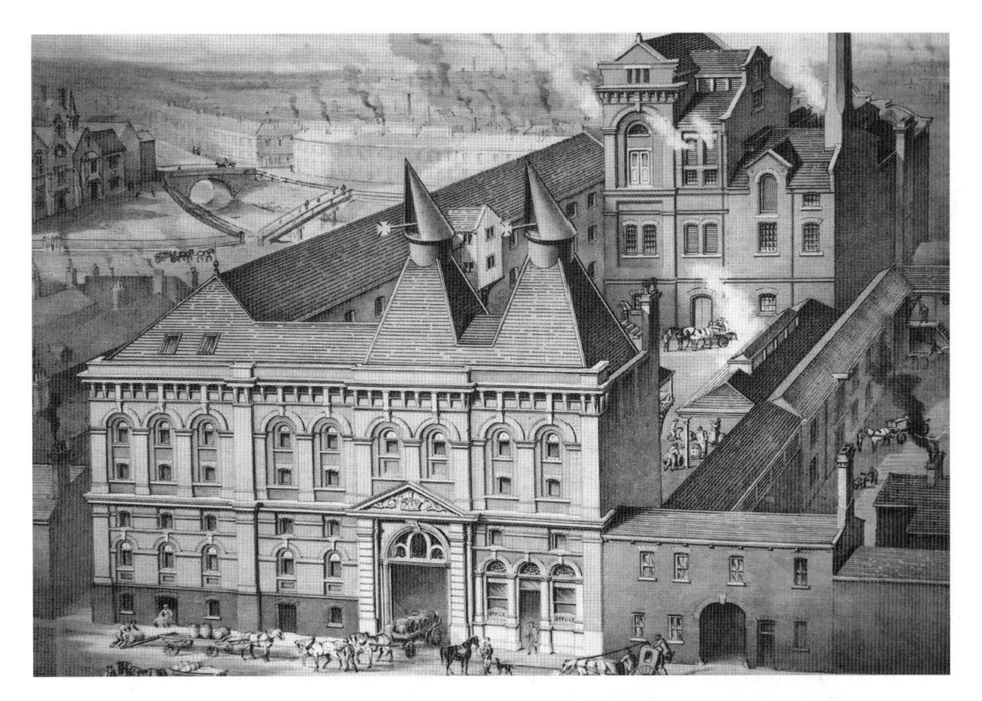

Hull's other large brewing company was that of Moors' & Robson's Ltd. Established in Raywell Street by 1848, latterly it had its own malt kilns. This is architect William Bradford's impression of the Crown Brewery as rebuilt in 1880. Only remnants of outbuildings and the 1912 offices survive in Francis Street.

Sadly few images survive of the brewery itself although some staff photographs have survived via the family of the photographer, Walter Robinson Burn. In a series of candid photographs taken in 1913, he captured the environment of the brewery and its staff.

Moors' & Robson's occupied various premises around Hull including a wine, spirit and bottled beer department in Sykes Street and the Newington Stores at No.453 Anlaby Road across from the Newington pub. Instantly recognisable by his smart uniform is another rully man standing proudly next to his vehicle.

Although working brewery lads may not have warranted the smart uniform of the rully man with his initialled cap and white jacket, the lads had a uniform of their very own; old sacks for aprons, waistcoats, collarless shirts and neckerchiefs.

Obviously management material, with his collar and tie, a white-collar worker stands with his young colleagues against hooped barrels in the yard.

No doubt the duties of these female staff were similar to those of the Hull Brewery Co. girls. They were possibly responsible for bottle washing and labelling duties. Labelling only became fully mechanised at Moors' & Robson's in 1949 following the installation of an automatic bottle labeller.

The rear of the Raywell Street brewery overlooked the Cottingham Drain and the houses of Richmond Terrace (the birthplace of the author). The warm by-products and waste from the brewery were let into the drain and members of my family can remember dangling their feet in the warm water. This lad was obviously on clean-up duties in the drain, with the shuttered houses of Richmond Terrace in the background.

Many breweries issued playing cards as part of their advertising material; the Hull Brewery Co. have seven known sets and Moors' & Robson's just one. The cartoonist Lawson Wood produced this illustration, which appeared on cards from the 1930s onwards. After the war small breweries were vulnerable to takeover from larger companies and in an attempt to prevent this Moors' & Robson's agreed to a friendly takeover bid from Hewitt's of Grimsby in 1960. Hewitt's retained their 320 licensed houses and acquired Moors' & Robson's 139. Sadly, Hewitt's were taken over by United Breweries in 1961 and the last 'brilliant beer' was brewed at the Crown Brewery in 1964.

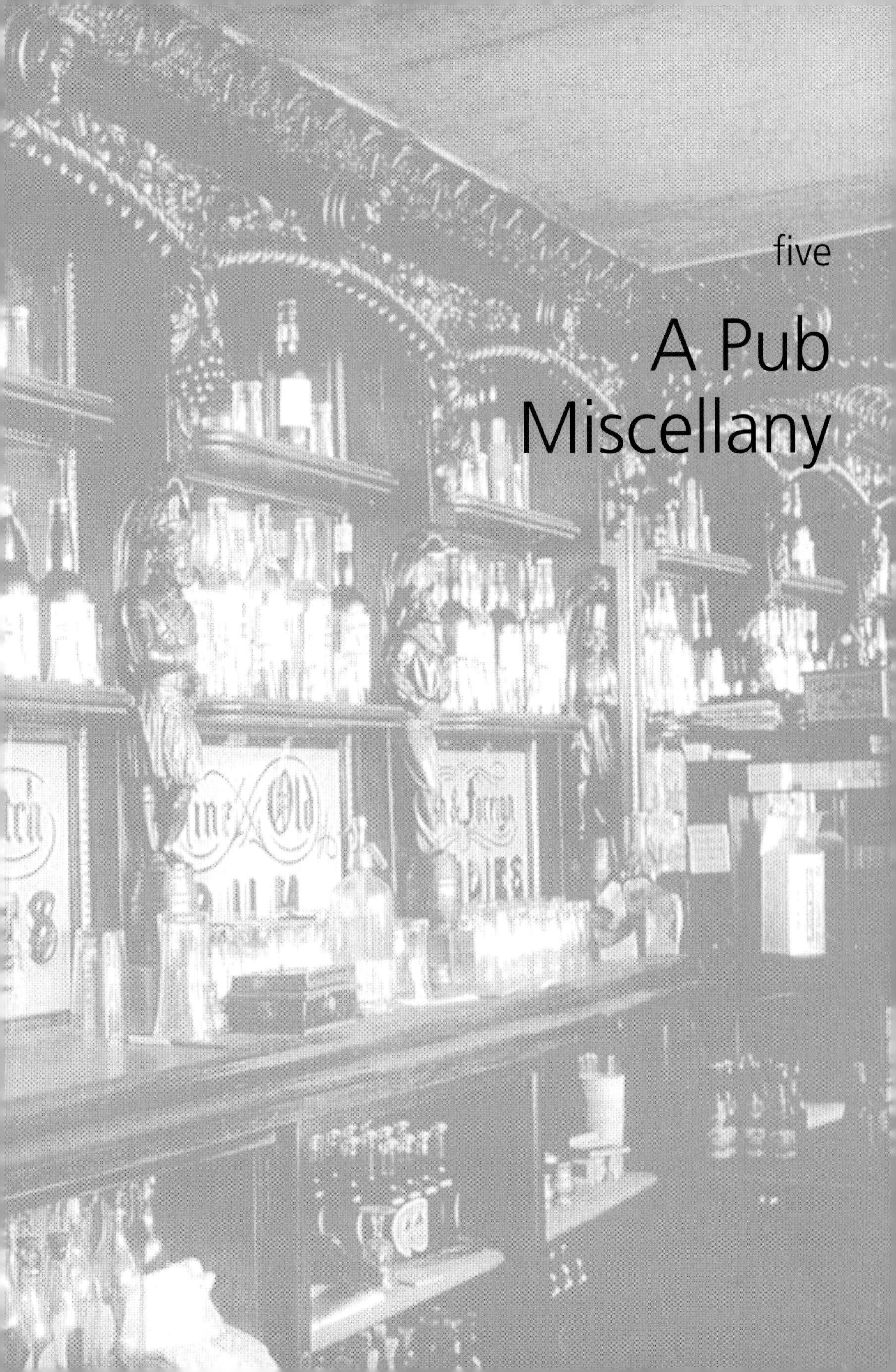

five

A Pub Miscellany

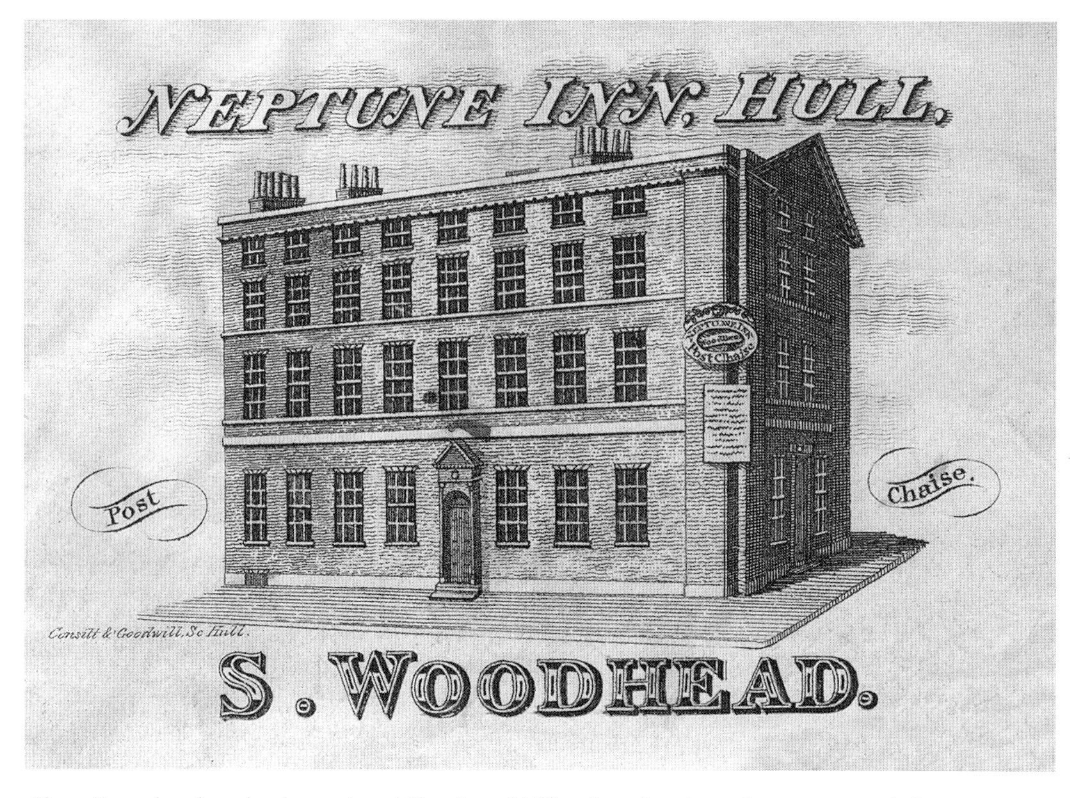

Above: Some hotels and pubs produced illuminated billheads and trade cards to promote their services. This is an early example from around 1823 for the Neptune Inn, on the corner of Chariot Street and Paragon Street. The Neptune, much rebuilt, survived until the 1940s (see p.77).

Opposite above: Directly opposite the Neptune was the Paragon Inn, shown here in an 1876 billhead. Notice the stable entrance on Chariot Street and the shop within the Paragon Street frontage which survived, somewhat altered into the 1970s.

Opposite below: Joseph Firth was licensee of the Punch Hotel from around 1850, and is noted as 'late of Wakefield' on this small advertisement from a local trade directory. The old Punch was rebuilt in 1895-96 (see p.24).

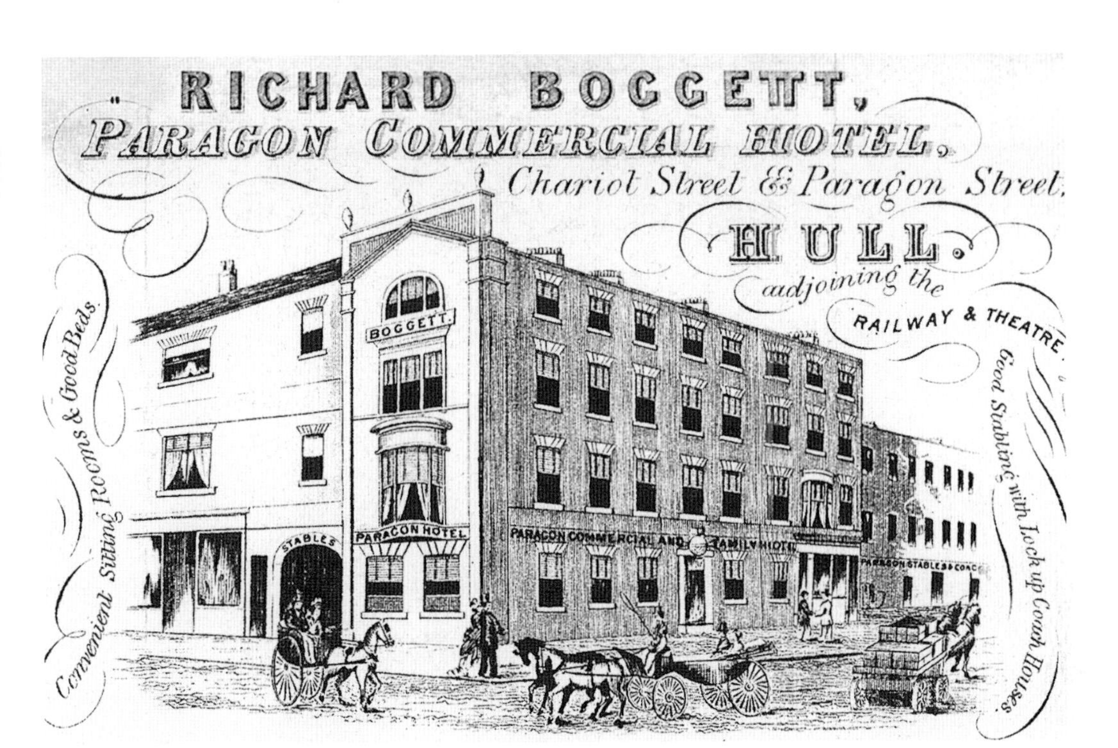
RICHARD BOGGETT,
PARAGON COMMERCIAL HOTEL,
Chariot Street & Paragon Street,
HULL.
adjoining the
RAILWAY & THEATRE.
Convenient Sitting Rooms & Good Beds.
Good Stabling with Lock up Coach Houses.
BOGGETT.
STABLES
PARAGON HOTEL
PARAGON COMMERCIAL AND FAMILY HOTEL

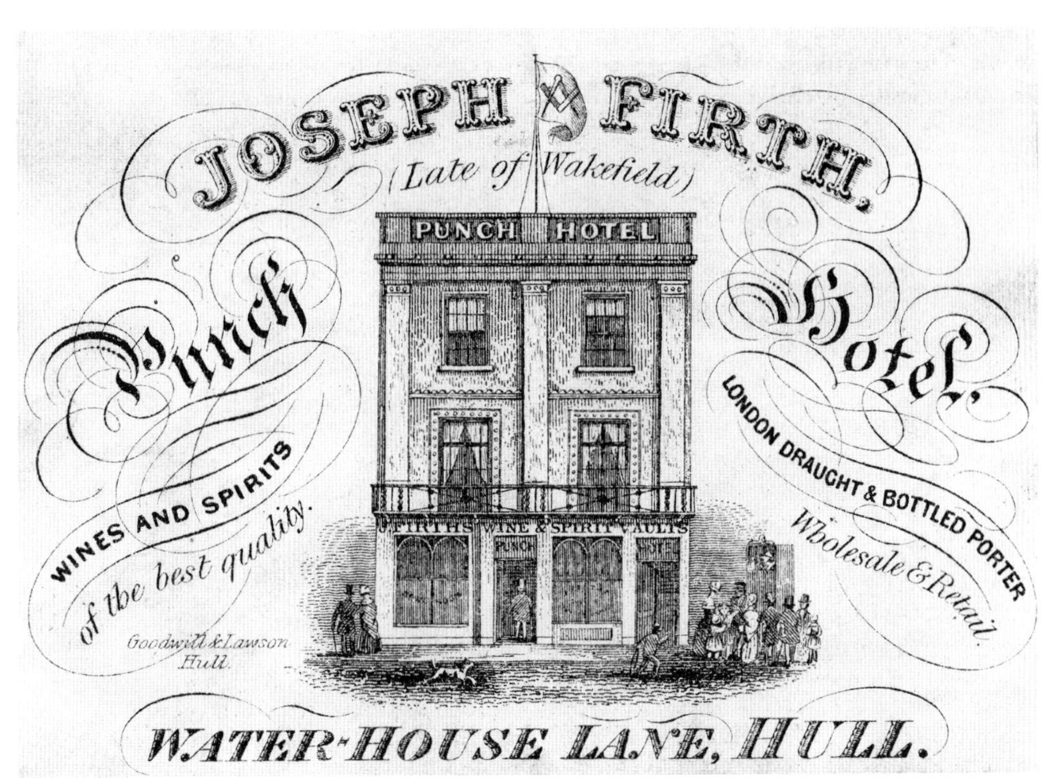
JOSEPH FIRTH,
(Late of Wakefield)
PUNCH HOTEL
Punch Hotel,
WINES AND SPIRITS
of the best quality.
LONDON DRAUGHT & BOTTLED PORTER
Wholesale & Retail.
FIRTHS WINE & SPIRIT VAULTS
PUNCH
Goodwill & Lawson
Hull.
WATER-HOUSE LANE, HULL.

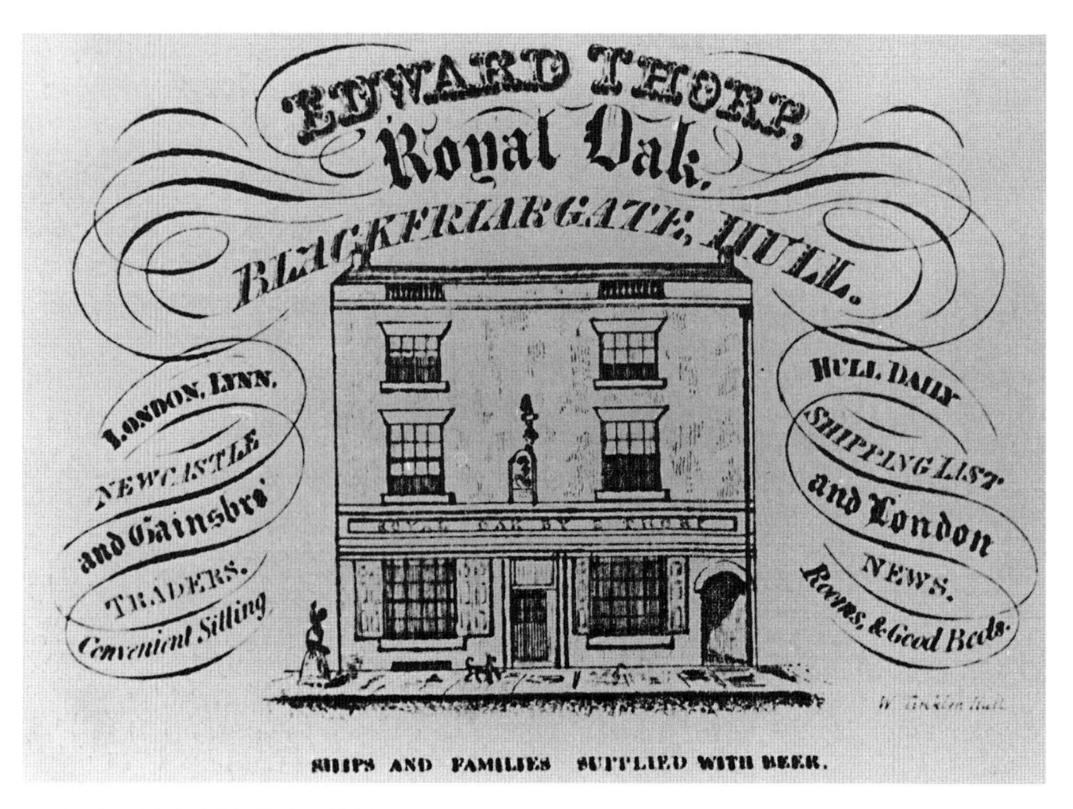

Above: Edward Thorp, licensee of the Royal Oak from 1826 until 1840, promoted his premises at No.42 Blackfriargate with this trade card, which notes 'Ships and families supplied with beer' and that newspapers and shipping lists were available. The Royal Oak closed in 1908.

Left: Charles Fox, was at the Flower Pot Inn, No.63 Whitefriargate from 1838 until around 1848. His pub (shown here in an advertisement from around the 1840s) was situated on the north side of Whitefriargate and closed in 1922. The site was redeveloped, initially as British Home Stores but is now Superdrug.

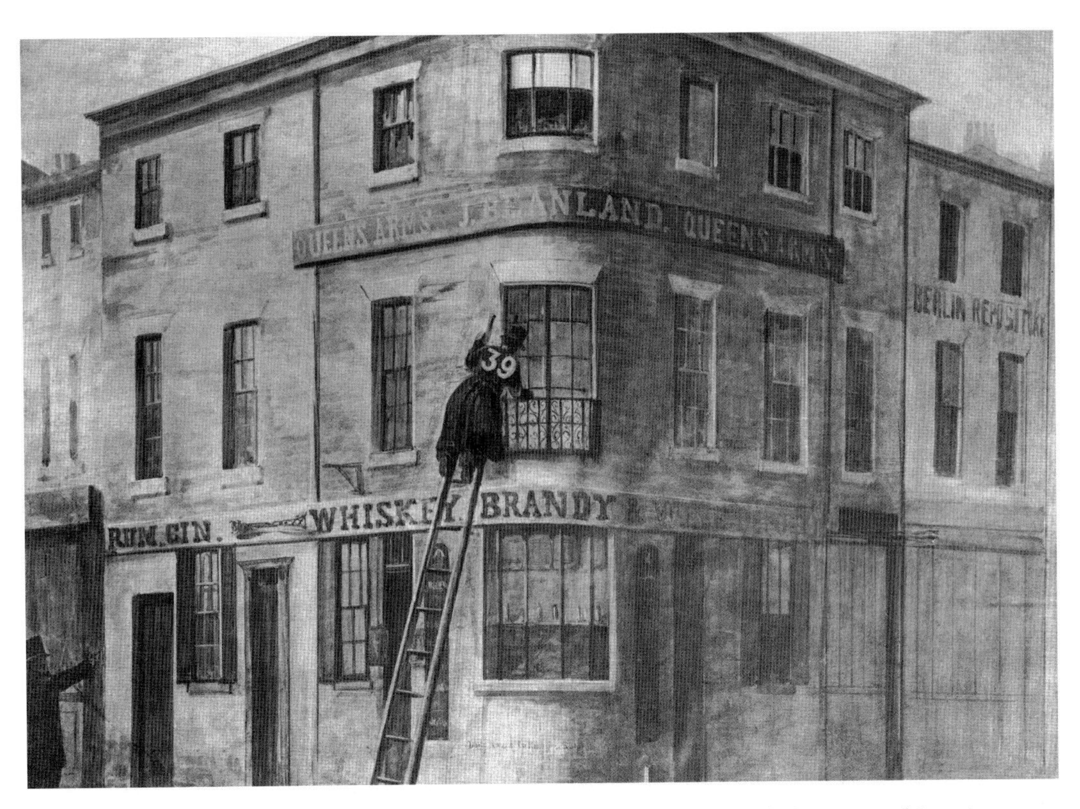

This drawing shows the Queens Arms, situated at the corner of St John's Street and Junction Street, now Victoria Square. Edmund Pettingell was the artist and the named licensee, J. Beanland, was at the pub until around 1858, which dates the view.

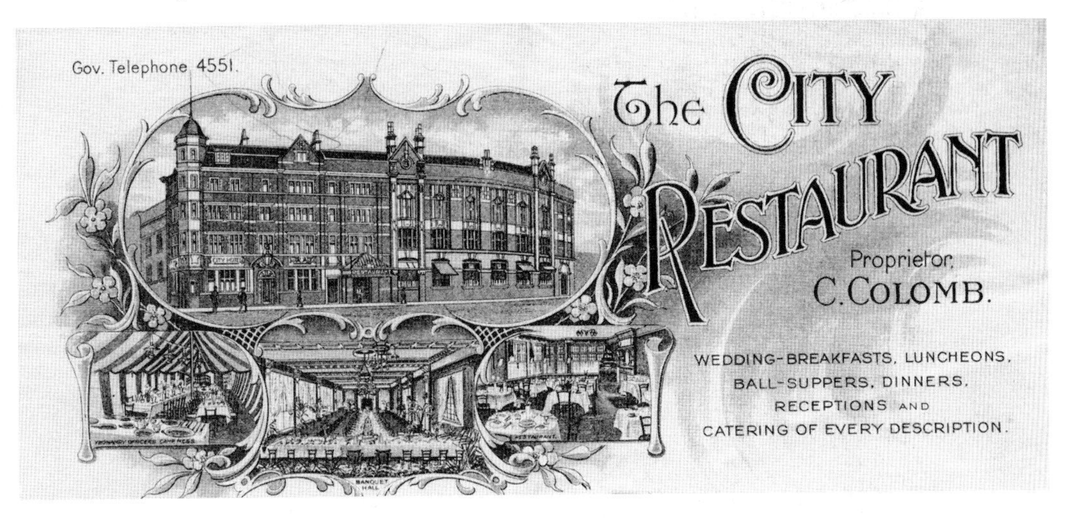

The City Hotel was rebuilt in 1903 following the construction of Alfred Gelder Street from around 1900. This billhead shows the hotel and the later restaurant that was built adjoining. Dated 1922 it was given as a receipt for £100 received in payment for a wedding reception, including all wines and food!

It had always been popular for group photographs to be taken outside pubs, usually of club or society outings. This group, just setting off in their charabanc, are outside the Oxford Inn around 1910. Situated on North Street (just next to the old Bladon's store) the Oxford closed in 1936.

A mixed group pose for the photographer at the rear of the Albany Hotel, Waterworks Street, shown here around 1905. Originally the Blue Bell it was renamed between 1885 and 1895 as the Albany Hotel (see p.52).

Above: Unmistakably 1920s fashion dominates this group, particularly the ladies' hats. Posing outside the Society Tavern, on the corner of Dagger Lane and Robinson Row the light from the east suggests that it is early morning and the group are on the way out for the day. The pub closed in 1961.

Right: Another popular subject for the local photographer was the small businessman outside his premises. Pub landlords featured in this genre and this is an example showing the Blue Bell Inn, No.110 Thomas Street, around 1900. The Blue Bell had been re-fronted in 1895 and closed in 1932.

The Ship Inn at No.21 Hodgson Street has served the residents of the Groves for almost 200 years. Shown here in the 1930s are licensee John Carver and his wife. Still trading today the Ship survives on the custom from many small businesses and light industry now dominating the area.

The Royal Hotel, No.54 Queen Street opened around 1830 and was owned for many years by Felix Woodruffe. Shown here around 1905 the property was on the corner of Wellington Street and closed in 1941 following blitz damage, the licence being transferred to the new Royal Hotel, Newbridge Road in 1949.

This is an early piece of trick photography produced for Billy Stonehouse, licensee of the South Myton Arms. Dated 1907, it is entitled *Waiting on Myself* and shows Billy at the rear of his pub being served by himself. The South Myton Arms, on the corner of St Luke's Street and Pease Street closed in 1939.

It is probably licensee David William Brown, with his wife and dog pictured outside the Windmill Hotel on Witham around 1915. Small bucket traps like these would have been a common sight on the streets of Hull at that time. Note the incredibly ornate windows of the Windmill, sadly lost during the Second World War.

Left and below: The position of licensee often held quite a place in Victorian society, depending on the type of premises. As such it was fitting to have a posed portrait produced by an eminent local photographer. This is William Bottomley, licensee of the Commercial Hotel Great Union Street, with members of his family around 1895. The Commercial was a busy pub, initially dealing with the many traders who came to market in Drypool and later with the huge number of workers in the factories that were built in the area. Shown here in the 1930s, the pub was badly damaged in the Second World War and was demolished soon after.

Above and below: To the far left in this photograph are the remains of the Lord Nelson pub, on the corner of Great Union Street and Witham, and further into the picture is the shell of the North Bridge Inn; both buildings having been devastated by bombing raids in 1941. The Nelson continued to trade (ground floor only!) until 1961 as shown in the photograph from the 1950s.

Hull was one of the most bombed cities in England during the Second World War. The Walker Arms on Jane Street is shown here following Blitz damage in 1942. The pub's licence was suspended following the damage, which was bad enough to force the closure of the pub.

Hull was also one of very few cities that was bombed during both world wars. Zeppelins loomed over Hull in 1916 and this view showing buildings in Queen Street shows the devastation caused. Shown centre-right is the former Golden Lion (see p.65) on the corner of Blanket Row, which closed following the air raid.

Above and right: This rare image shows the interior of the original White Lion on Collier Street. The building was lost in the demolition for the new Ferensway and bus station around 1930 but at that time Hull Museums were acquiring material for a mock-up of an old street, to be housed in the Wilberforce Museum. All of these fittings were saved and placed in a reproduction tavern in the fictional street. Sadly, the street and most of its irreplaceable contents were destroyed during the Blitz of the Second World War. The old White Lion is shown here in the 1920s; the new White Lion opened in Lombard Street in 1934 (see p.92).

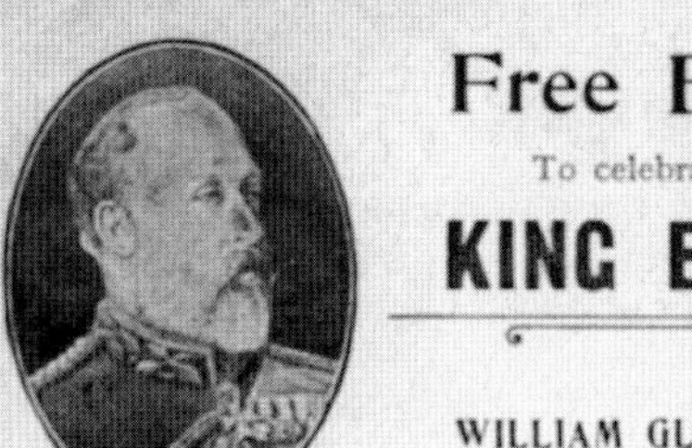

4922

Free Beer Ticket

To celebrate the Coronation of

KING EDWARD VII.

ISSUED BY

WILLIAM GLOSSOP & BULAY, Ltd.,

BREWERS, HULL.

To the Landlord of any House named on the back.

Globe Brewery, Hull, June 18th, 1902.

Please supply Bearer with one pint of best beer, free, on either June 26th or 27th, to drink the health of their Majesties.

For **Wm. GLOSSOP & BULAY, Ltd.**

Ticket to be handed to the Landlord for retention.

A. Bulay Glossop

Above: William Glossop & Bulay Ltd, were another of Hull's brewers, their Globe Brewery founded in Lincoln Street in 1833 continued to brew until at least 1902. This Free Beer Ticket was issued to celebrate the coronation of King Edward VII.

Left: From around 1840, many pubs issued coins known as pub checks; these were mostly produced in Birmingham and not legal tender, but could be used at the pub in which they were issued. Ceasing to be used in the early twentieth century, at least nine are known to exist for Hull. The example shown here was issued for the Oxford Inn, North Street around 1900.

Above: This card is an example of the promotional items that were produced by hotels and pubs before the advent of today's glossy brochures. The Grosvenor Hotel (see p.69) could boast '66 bedrooms, sitting rooms, 8 stock rooms, restaurant, billiard room (2 tables), coffee rooms, commercial rooms, and a ladies drawing room' and the modern convenience of 'electric light in every room of the building'.

Right: Many late nineteenth-century pubs produced bottles or flasks with the pub's details embossed upon them and appear to have been used in Hull up until 1920, but rarely after. Shown here is an example from the Dover Castle, Norfolk Street.

Left and below: Hull, long without a brewery of its own, now has a new micro-brewery; the Whalebone Brewery in Wincolmlee. Once one of many pubs serving the Greenland Whaling yards of the area, the Whalebone was established around 1800. The current landlord and real ale fan Alex Craig and his wife Tina came to the Whalebone in 2002 and set up the brewery in 2003. The first brew, Neck Oil, was served in July of that year and is literally going from strength to strength; the brewery is now selling beer as far afield as Manchester. Latest brews, all following the whaling theme, include: Moby Dick, Diana Mild and Truelove Porter.

An interesting pastime when out and about is discovering the old remains of logos and initials from defunct Hull breweries on pubs around Hull. Obviously better after a pint on a summer evening or Sunday afternoon, it is not difficult once you get your eye tuned in. Look for anchors within ceramic tile-work and in stone detailing, and M&R in stone or ironwork. It is even possible to see reminders of out of town breweries, for example, Hewitt's and Darley's. Good examples can be found at:

Alexandra, Hessle Road – Hull Brewery Co. anchor logo in tiled panel over door
Blacksmith's Arms, Naylors Row – Darley's armoured horse logo in tiled corner panel
Dairycoates Inn, Hessle Road – Hull Brewery Co. tiled anchor logo (shown above)
Fiveways, Boothferry Road – M&R symbol in window railings
Inkerman Tavern, Alfred Street – M&R stone detail over door
Lambwath, Sutton Road – M&R rainwater heads and incised stone details
Marrowbone & Cleaver, Hotham Road North – Hull Brewery Co. mosaic tiled logo
Mr Q's, Ferensway – M&R rainwater heads
Polar Bear, Spring Bank – Hull Brewery Co. anchor logo in stone detail
Punch, Queen Victoria Square – Hull Brewery Co. terracotta logo
Red Lion, Clarence Street – M&R rainwater heads and incised initials in wall decoration
Yorkshireman, Lombard Street – M&R rainwater heads and window railings

If this book has sparked any interest in pubs and pub architecture then there are some pubs you must see. If you never look closely at any other pubs, I would suggest that you visit the following this year. Don't just look at the outside – go in for a pint (unless you're driving) and look for any details that are old or original. Do be aware however that wonderful exteriors can often hide a multitude of modern sins within. A walk around the Old Town should include the following:

Start at the **City Hotel**, opposite the Guildhall in Alfred Gelder Street. This is one of the pubs in Hull with Art Nouveau details. Travel east towards the river and be surprised why you've never looked closer at, or even been in, the **White Hart** (see p.28). Cross the road, entering High Street, and head south until you reach the **Black Boy**, at No.150 High Street – a listed building, serving real ales (see p.16). Continue along High Street before turning right into Scale Lane, passing the ornate exterior of the **Manchester Arms** on your left, before heading for the Market Place at the end of the street. Don't be surprised when you don't see a market – it moved many years ago – cross the road and look for a large blue bell at the entrance to a passage, at the end of which you will find the **Blue Bell**, (see p.14) one of only two Samuel Smith's pubs in the city. Now is an excellent time to catch your breath and have a pint with your lunch. After retracing your steps along the passage turn right towards the Holy Trinity Church, turning right into North Chuch Side, notice the exterior woodwork of the **Corn Exchange** (see p.14) with its heads of Ceres, the Roman goddess of Corn. At the end of North Church Side you will find the **Kingston**; one of Hull's earliest gin palace-style pubs (see p.21). Turn right into Trinity House Lane and cross directly into Land of Green Ginger, noticing on your left the **George**; the vaults of the former George Coaching Inn (see p.15). Look out for the tiny window once used by the night watchman to inspect those wanting entry through the coaching arch to the stables. Cross the road and enter Bowlalley Lane, on the right-hand side of which you will see the White Hart symbol over a gated access to a passage. Enter the passage and travel back in time to the **Old White Hart**, Hull's oldest pub building (see p.11).

On another day try these central and western pubs. You may need a street map and either a driver or your bike:

Start at the **Punch**, Victoria Square – a listed building (see p.24) and move on via the **Paragon** (Hull Cheese) Paragon Street a late 1880s gin palace. Cross into Jameson Street and find the **Master's Bar** (formerly the Waverley Hotel) a listed building, with one of the best exteriors in the new town area (of 1903 by Freeman Son & Gaskell). Head west for Ferensway and once reached turn south and across the busy Mytongate/Castle Street junction after examining the **Earl De Grey** (shown opposite) to the east. As you enter Commercial Road you will see the impressive exterior of the **Whittington** from around 1902. Returning to the busy junction turn west on to Hessle Road passing the **Vauxhall Tavern** (see p.17) and look out for the **Alexandra** (see p.25) another listed building. Pass under the Daltry Street flyover and carry on along the Hessle Road. Here you will find the **Star & Garter**, the **Criterion** (see p.21), the **Halfway House** (see p.22) finishing with the superb tiled exterior of the **Dairycoates Inn** (see p.19).

Space does not permit other possible routes, but try to include the following on other trips: Starting at the **Polar Bear**, Spring Bank, take in the **St John's,** Queen's Road – (see p.19); the **Bull**, Beverley Road – a listed building (see p.27); the **Swann**, Beverley Road and of course the **Whalebone**, Wincolmlee – Hull's only brewery (see p.124).

Or, starting at the **Windmill**, Witham – (see p.25) then head for the **Plimsoll**, Witham (see p.20) and a really good clutch of early nineteenth-century pubs and small beerhouses in Drypool – the **Victoria Dock Tavern**, Great Union Street (see p.18); the **Victoria**, old Hedon Road and the **Duke of Edinburgh**, Great Union Street (see p.18).

Happy drinking, and Cheers!

The Earl De Grey, a listed building, has recently re-opened and is enjoying renewed success.

Other local titles published by Tempus

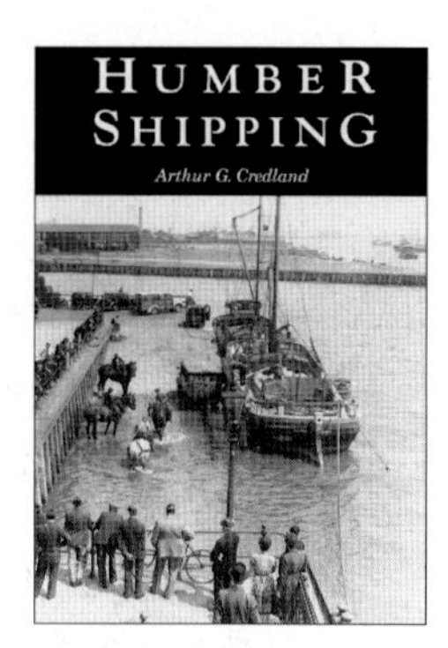

Humber Shipping

ARTHUR G. CREDLAND

Kingston upon Hull has been a major port since medieval times, and over a long period the city grew to be one of Britain's major ports and shipbuilding centres. Today the Humber looks much different than it did even ten years ago. Many docks and warehouses have gone and the fishing fleet is greatly reduced. Illustrated with over 200 images *Humber Shipping* reveals the changing face of the Humber's maritime history.

0 7524 2358 4

Hull Speedway 1930-81

ROGER HULBERT

Kingston upon Hull is best known for the Rugby League exploits of its two professional teams. However, speedway has also established a place in the city's sporting history, and the team has performed at the top level of British speedway. The club has boasted four World Champions in its rider roster, including Ivan Mauger, Barry Briggs and Sam Ermolenko. This book includes comprehensive statistical information and many rare pictures.

0 7524 3200 1

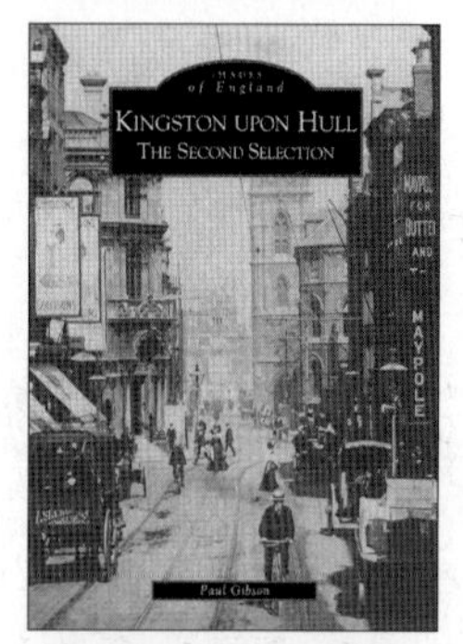

Kingston upon Hull The Second Selection

PAUL GIBSON

Kingston upon Hull is a city of great variety and contrast, including docks, industry, civic buildings and residential areas. This selection of archive images brings to life many of the streets and long-forgotten work places that have disappeared or have changed beyond recognition, and rekindles many nostalgic memories for those who remember how the city used to be.

0 7524 2607 9

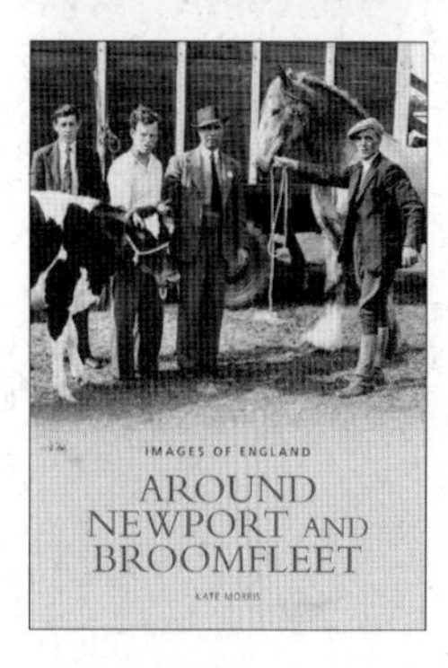

Around Newport and Broomfleet

KATE MORRIS

Around Newport and Broomfleet is a pictorial history of the communities at River Bridge on the banks of the Market Weighton Canal. The volume recalls life as it once was in Newport and its surrounding villages, including Broomfleet, Faxfleet and Brantingham. Compiled with over 150 archive images, this collection features important buildings and places of worship, transport and local businesses, as well as the people who lived and worked here.

0 7524 3126 9

If you are interested in purchasing other books published by Tempus, or in case you have difficulty finding any Tempus books in your local bookshop, you can also place orders directly through our website

www.tempus-publishing.com